CHRONICLES OF THE WEEPING ADDICTS

A Manual For Creative Souls

Author: J.I. Brown

Contributions by: R.K. Chohan

Copyright © 2016 J.I. Brown

All rights reserved.

ISBN: 10:0692700803

ISBN-13: 13:978-0692700808

*Soon you and I will climb
Make it through the storms and fly
Spread your wings and I'll spread mine
Together high in the sky.*

Dedicated to Mom, Dad, and you, the reader.

CONTENTS

Preface…………………………………………....	01
Recovery Awareness Guide……………………..	05
Addiction Would Have You…………………..	13
Sandra's Lost: Level 1……………………………...	23
Luis And Lust: Level 2…………………………..	27
Kristian's Nightmare: Level 3…………………………	31
NEFTWD……………………………………………..	35
NEFTWD Follow Up………………………………..	37
Faded Dreams: Level 1…………………………..	39
Only On Special Occasions: Level 2………………..	43
Needle In A Haystack: Level 3……………………..	47
The Supplier: Level 4……………………………….	53
Float Forward: Level 5……………………………...	57

Facts…………………………………………..	59
In A New Light………………………………..	65
My Beginnings………………………………..	67
LA Experience………………………………..	71
Guilt…………………………………………..	87
Consequence………………………………….	91
Strength…………………………………….....	99
Breaking the Cycle……………………….…..	103
Rehab, "The Hab...	111
Environment……………………………….…..	109
Amazing Life…………………………………..	111
Brighter Days…………………………….…....	113

PREFACE

Addiction has been like a family member that I've grown to hate but know very well. I grew up in an outstanding, dysfunctional home, and all I wanted was to get away from the madness, but it stalked me every fucking where I went. It was on every street corner, at every musical event, and especially around me when I was at my lowest. To be frank, those around me offered it to me like I was sick and in need of medicine. I was sick, but that was the wrong type of fucking medicine. Listening, sharing, reading, and writing are the types of medicine that have helped me comprehend addiction, dysfunctionality, and recovery. The power of my stories and others' I have crossed during my journey to recovery have been priceless lessons in my life.

I want to help people realize their potential fully. No matter how hard you have failed in the past, you can still pick yourself up and try again. We are not losers, we are winners. Addiction is a suffocating veil that's blinding us from our greatness. I know you are great. Some people who were "close" to me saw that greatness within me but didn't want me to soar because misery loves company. They wanted to keep me around that lifestyle and then shun me when I tried to do things differently. I wandered around like a chicken with its head cut off, while my so-called friends played soccer with the detached head.

    The universe was throwing every obstacle in my way, but I managed to surmount them by learning to believe in myself and unwiring those negative thinking patterns. I went out and started learning. I learned how to take care of myself, not just physically, but spiritually and emotionally. I had to combat my negative habits with expansion of the mind and inner growth. I felt like my environment became too little for me to continuously grow. The people I was around brought others down, including myself. They talked about all their goals, but never took action to realize them and complained about the way they were living.

    I found myself in that gap and was completely aware of it, but I became stuck with a lot of my past's baggage. I lost my father, I drank and went crazy. I lost my mother, I drank and went crazy. I was in a dark place, and I desperately wanted to get out. It had come to life and death. I was silently suffering, but I slowly started telling people that I was an alcoholic even though it was obvious that I had a problem. When I did confess my truth, compassion was lacking from family members as though it was my problem alone. The only attention that came from my alcoholism was gossip. Assumptions were always made even by family that I was doing real bad. They never took the time to find out my truth as to why I was suffering. I had to fend for myself. I painstakingly erased people who were unfit for my recovery. It was painful because I loved them and they had a fucked up way of loving me back.

    What I ultimately learned from all this is you have to let go. Let go of your expectations of others. Let people in who are worth your love and trust. My therapist asked me who I considered family and asked me to list the first words that came to my mind when I thought of the word family. My list was 98% negative connotations. I thought of the fact that I didn't have parents anymore, and she said to me that my family could be whoever I want them to be. They don't have to be related by blood. From that eye-opening statement, I felt powerful. I had forgotten that I am the creator. I can pick and choose who I want in my pretty freaking amazing life. All the toxic relationships I had, I broke away from.

I wanted to write this book to let you know that you are not alone and that some people don't have the capacity to help those who are in a rut because that's just what they choose not to do or because they don't know how to help. We can be strong together, and we can surround ourselves with people who get it. We don't have to wait for people to see us because we are going to start to see ourselves. Those who choose not to see will only miss out on the wonderful transformation. I see you, somewhere in the distance.

I have learned so much about patience, persistence, and the force of strength in this process. Willingness and openness to possibilities are key to metamorphosis. My learning doesn't stop where I am now. I have a lot of soul searching and knowledge to gain. I have come to an understanding that the outside environment doesn't change, it is you who changes.

People are going to do what they want to do and there is no point in creating suffering because they may not understand you. Action has to be taken by talking about addiction and the causes of addiction that hit closest to home. For instance, trauma, depression, childhood neglect, the availability of noxious substances to minors. The list can go on and on, but my point is that we have to stop pretending that things are okay when things are in fact not.

As you read this book I would like you to keep in mind the Recovery Awareness Guide. I want your objective from here on out to be able to keep your head above water, metaphorically speaking. Do not drown in life, and remember that you are worth taking care of yourself because you *love* yourself. You are not alone, the sun is shining somewhere in the world and eventually it will shine down upon you. When you wake up in the morning, you are able to start fresh. I believe that you can become what you want to become. You are unique and special. Be excited about your life, you are in control.

RECOVERY AWARENESS GUIDE

      Support is great! Think of it as a gift. Friend to friend, brother to brother, sister to sister, family member to family member, even stranger to stranger. My suggestion would be to accept, unwrap, and take what you possibly can from that gift. Once opened you may find advice, cheers, *you can do its*, and those *everything's going to be okays*. Thank them for their encouragement and try your hardest to apply what you've gained from them. There are crickets in the room! Encouragement from outside sources can only last so long, but how would I know? I've walked in numerous shoe sizes, that's how.

      Society has forgotten their power. Support begins with regrouping, but we must understand our individual core, our burning like essence. We cannot be ignorant because ignorance is time-consuming and similarly, so is awakening. Awakening is time well managed and time well spent. You are nothing more and nothing less than who you are choosing to be right now! Although it may seem foggy and you can barely see ahead, just think that one step forward vibrates ecosystems.

That vibration is epic. Every single step forward not only affects your life but those around you, even species the naked eye can't possibly see. We all have quirks, tendencies, and habitual ways. Let's hold tight to the positive and wash away as much filth as we can. Can you sleep in a pissy bed? Can you eat in a dirty kitchen? Can you work in a cluttered office? Can you concentrate, even operate in chaos? Addiction is hysteria.

One morning, I'm not going to say I had just awakened because I'd been awake all night telling myself to fall asleep, the emotions I had felt made me more sluggish and drained. I could not understand why I was so fucking irritable, angry, sad, and frustrated all at once. I started to see white dots and my eyes were heavy. My heart could not stop racing. I seriously felt like I was slipping away. My hand held my head up slightly, and I said aloud, "I feel like I'm trying to keep my head above water." Wow! My invisible light bulb came shining brightly on. What a great metaphor! Picture, imagine this. Close your eyes. Further explaining awaits shortly.

You are at the beach, a beautiful serene beach. You are standing. Birds are flying around you. It's not too hot, nor too cold. The temperature is right in between. The sun soothes your skin. The waves are like musical tunes. Now start walking towards the beautiful shore. Towards the water. Feel the sand beneath your feet. Notice the gritty sensation. Take a deep breath. The remanence of a wave just hit your feet. You decide to go further. Ah, the cool water touches your knees. You like this feeling so you continue. Now the water is gripping your waist. You slowly walk through the water inches deeper.

Suddenly, an unexpected dip! Now the water sends chill bumps radiating through and through you. The ocean's water reaches your chest. A wave is coming. The water doesn't have you still anymore. You are losing control now. The wave hits. Swoosh. The backlash pull has water up to your throat. You are struggling now. Your feet are wandering through floating ocean debris. You begin to tread water frantically. All you see is vast ocean, wide from every angle. You don't know what's beneath or around you in this water. Shivers are your last concern. Salt water smacks against your lips. You have had a taste of the ocean. Too much to bare. Cannot withstand. Your muscles are shutting down. In an instant, your strength retreats. Unbelievable. You are drowning now. Head is below. Finished. Done. Gone.

Are you treading water or are you drowning?

The first step is awareness. The recovery awareness guide was created in hopes of helping the individual notice their states of negative feelings and well-being. Pay attention to the negative feelings you may feel that play a huge part in whether you drown or stay afloat. The levels are in order from low functioning to high functional serenity.

The first two levels are intense negative emotions to be wary of when they jolt up.

Level 1- ***Drowning***: hopeless, despair, giving in, personal imprisonment, unbearable depression, lost, dead-ends, negative cycles consumes. Stress disguises as diseases and distortion. Destruction is prevalent.

Level 2- **Head above water**: exhaustion, dilemma, questioning, anger, high anxiety, insomnia, tension, caught in between fighting and giving up (swimming and sinking).

In the next set, you can be fully present with what you are experiencing, yet you may find yourself experiencing previous low functioning levels.

Level 3- **Water to your chest**: dismay, anticipation, reality comes in clear view.

Level 4- **Water to your waist**: risking, spontaneous, fluid, inspired, energetic, focused, fearful.

Now in the final level, all is well, but it may be hard to get here because of *fear*. The fear in being someone better and different than what you think you have become used to. However, you must delve deep into courage to get here.

Level 5- **Water to your feet**: relaxed, settled, accomplished, self-aware, loving oneself, opening heart, freedom, purity, cleansed, able to love, awake, peace, contentment, reasoning, clarification, evolved, elation.

Once you become aware of the level you find yourself in, use the following Recovery Awareness Tips:

Level 1 Tips: Our goal, our objective, plain and simple, is to not drown in life. Drowning can and will not be an option. Let's have a clear view on what sends you in that direction of possibly drowning. What triggers your personal imprisonment? What triggers your feelings of despair? Why are you in Level 1? It is up to you to find a path of coping mechanisms. I would suggest writing thoughts down to quiet your brain a bit. Start with goal setting. Once reached you may feel a sense of accomplishment. This is a great start to awareness and recovery.

Level 2 Tips: Try finding new ways to soothe your soul. Explore the never seen and the never attempted. Create new habits, instead of walking down the same street, walk the one that's a little lengthier. You already know what's down the street that you have walked down countless times before. Most likely you will see the same people, the same *negative* people who will keep you hostage in your destructive behavior. They are distractions!

Pay attention to your surroundings. Notice what you have not noticed before. It could be something as minuscule as a yellow sunflower sprouting in the crack of a cemented pavement. Strike back at your anxiety by stepping forward proudly that you made it this far. Tell yourself, "I can do this!" Try drinking chamomile tea at night before bed. Lavender essential oils can help with relaxation. Also, deep breathing, visualization, and hot baths are among my favorite soothing practices.

Level 3 Tips: Pay close attention to what you are feeling and what's happening to you. Prepare yourself for what you have put out into the complex system. Affirm to yourself that you are okay and everything will be just fine. Also, try creating affirmations of all your good qualities and what

you aspire to do. Write it with the intention that you *will do* something or as it has *already* been done. You have to believe! Carry on with faith, whatever faith you relate with.
Level 4 Tips: Accept your moment. Do something that brings positive joy in your life. Do what they said you could not do. Seize the day. Embrace! Speak with someone you would never think you would gain insight from. Explore new notions and new talents. Take on endeavors and new challenges. You are doing great!

Level 5 Tips: If no one else does, congratulate yourself. At the end of the day, this is what matters, that you give yourself credit. Set time aside to think of all you have done to get to this point. You have done the work and have passed strenuous tests. You have been conditioned. You should be proud and secure with what you have become.

You are unmovable. Take a breather. Life does get better after the tumultuous struggle. The rain eventually clears up. Flowers eventually bloom. Recognize this moment. Cherish it and be thankful for all you have even when others may think you have absolutely nothing. This life is all you own, you are the pilot. You are the driver. You are the individual in the arena. You are in control!

Yes, we are in control but we must be honest with ourselves. Some people will never admit because they are too ashamed, or too embarrassed and afraid. That fear radiates every fiber, every cell inside and outside your body. A disease so disordered penetrates through flesh like hookworms. Taking over your body, invading your body, setting up shop, and consuming all energy until your soul retreats. This is not only a nightmare, but a battlefield. You are at war! Are you equipped?

For those who neglect, shimmy around with their tails between their legs, you have some extensive conditioning to make time for. You have to wake up! Your vital organs are depending on you. Find your purpose. Do not think you are here just because and that there is no need for your presence. You cannot be an imbecile! Honesty shall set you free. Do not run away from yourself.

Are we addicted to pain, saddened emotions, insanity as well? How many times must we bump our heads, or play with fire to notice that this shit does hurt? Why must we continue a cycle that leads back to where we left off? Take a look around, what emotions do you feel? Are you at the bottom yet? Can't breathe from the suffocation? Are you too cool, too hip, or arrogant to change? Are you worried what your so-called "friends" would say when you shift gears without a signal and you drive off and turn a different way?

Go ahead and let them keep bumping heads until they get the colossal knot. Let them play with fire until they become ash. All bullshit to the side. No one cares about you, but if you are lucky you might have a chance. Snakes creep up and in. It does not matter if it is day, evening, or night. You have to be equipped at any and every moment. It is only a matter of time before they strike. Infecting you with the deadliest venom. They are miserable without you. Envious that you had the courage to even say you have had enough.

There is absolutely no room for drama. Are you getting paid to act out in it? Didn't think so. You have lost yourself in this maze we call life. Forget, become numb to those who enable you in your destructive behavior. Never once think you are powerless. Let go and master your heart, body, and brain. If you are afraid right now, close this book and put yourself on time out. You most definitely need to change your mindset, your perception of your life. The following should give you an idea on why this necessary change is urgent.

ADDICTION WOULD HAVE YOU

Addiction would have you curled up in fetal position
Terrified
Addiction would have you broke and evicted
Wondering
What the hell really happened…
Addiction would have you lost in blank thought
Addiction would have you sleep on public transportation
'till closing
Addiction would have you hitchhiking in the early mornings
Addiction would have you in the back of police vehicles on the way to county
But be damned lucky if they actually took your ass home
Addiction would have you
Punched

Bitch slapped
Cussed out
Dragged out of Hollywood hotels by security, bleeding
Addiction would have you looking stupid as fuck
Singing hallelujahs in the middle of intersections
While sports cars maneuver around you
Addiction would have you either permanent or temporarily psychotic
Addiction would have you with lost limbs and bullet wounds
Addiction would have you forgetting to eat, pee, even defecate
Addiction would have you locked up
But too dumb enough to conjure up an escape
Addiction would have you feeling blue with no friends or grown kids to even run to
Addiction would have you driving drunk
Hitting parked cars
Flipping over and leaving with only a bruise
Addiction would have you feeling invulnerable, indomitable, unconquerable
Basically invincible
Addiction would have you teary eyed from vanished dreams
Addiction would have you reminiscing about those once upon a times
Addiction would have you unemployed
Shit out of luck with only your drug of choice to enjoy
Addiction would have you confused about what day of the week it is
Wednesday
But
Monday you had business to tend to
Addiction would have you begging for
Change
Clothes

And
Shoes
Addiction would have you in midnight alleys
Lying in trash debris
Surrounded by flesh eating rats
Used needles and prostitutes
Addiction would have you living with regrets
Addiction would have you bleeding profusely
Getting tattoos half finished
Addiction would have you stale
Rotten
Discombobulated
Barely functioning properly far from orderly
Addiction would have you searching for
God
Allah
Buddha
Dalai Lama,
Alternative medicines
Past boyfriends or girlfriends
Addiction would have you facing mirrors with distorted
reflections
Consumed and flooded
Guilt and embarrassment
Sheds light onto your soul
Addiction would have you trembling
Heart pounding from chest
Well
That is the heart that you have left
Addiction would have you
Nauseated
Gagging
Paranoid
That everyone can see
When no one, really no one gives a fuck

Addiction would have you sober for two days to rid
hangovers
Addiction would have you drinking just to "cure"
hangovers
Catch 22
Addiction would have you cracking brandy 5ths in the
cereal isle at Foods Co.
Addiction would have you drinking on 15 minute breaks in
your company's restroom
Addiction would have you using all your colognes and
perfumes
Still reeking from pores
The trident commercial didn't do what it was supposed to
Dammit
Addiction would have you substituting one for the other
Addiction would have you in
Gurneys
Ambulances
On your second I.V.
Addiction would have you waking up with strangers and
wanting to leave ASAP
Addiction would have you
Divorced
Splitting assets
Addiction would have you faintly panting
Struggling to hold on
Addiction would have you slowly turning Alaskan cold
Suddenly your lips turn blackish purple
Eyes dilate
Contract
Surrounding sound loses its reverberation
Five senses gone within milliseconds
Spirit emerges
Lighter than air
In-between
Limbo

The energy still lingers
You probably slipped away in another addict's fingers
Strong pull
This life force will not change the course of your direction
now
Floating on black clouds
Tears are raindrops now
What legacy did you leave?
Who did you love?
Who loved you?
Addiction would have you
Gasping for air...
As you are engulfed by dark, cold waves...

I am sure that poem rings a bell so loud and clear. It is the insanity of addiction. Are you willing to change for the better and rewrite your journey? You may be anxious to start and you may be fearful. Albeit, fear exists within us, it is a natural reflex when we notice danger, but bravery and courage follow right after, that is if you choose to be the hero in your precious life. Every person on this planet grows from an infant, pre-teen, teen, and so forth. Our outwards appearance does not depict who we really are. However, we are extremely focused on how we look. What if we were turned inside out? Would we be as concerned as to what others may think of us? That would be just letting it all hang out, right?

Likely we would feel bare, exposed, and fragile. However, we could then look in our mirrors and see what needs to be reconstructed. We have neglected what we could not see but noticed the pain while unable to pinpoint the exact area where it slowly penetrated. We eventually ignored it until we became immune. Every day we wake up and take for granted the air we are so privileged to be receiving. We go out in the world creating our reality, our outcomes. We get what we put out in our complex system.

The day will bring some type, some sort of challenge. You must conquer every situation that tries to persuade you in directions of resentment. There will be triggers that will send you back to the pain you felt that you could not pinpoint. Maybe it is a good time to wear your heart on your sleeves. How could you be fearful if the unexpected already happened to you? The problems arise with attachments to past failures and expectations of future failures or pain. You lost the game, now it's time to reevaluate, try again, and proceed.

Proceed inside out. Become selfish, self-centered because the only person that needs you is you right now. If you had the means and knowledge to heal your wound before it became infected, wouldn't you heal it before you would heal someone else's wound? How the hell can you help them when you are bleeding to death without much strength? Fix yourself first and then you can help others. Maintain your body's awesome chemistry.

Keep your necessary items, e.g., water, food, clothes on your back, toothpaste, soap, medicines, etc. All the other crap, such as negative people and unnecessary material distractions, do not play a part in your life right now. Really realize that all you have left in your life is whom you see when facing the mirror. Go stand in front of a mirror. Who do YOU see when you are stripped of people, material belongings, and past memories that you have allowed to identify who you are as an individual?

It is vital that you rejuvenate. Shed layers of dead skin, and bring forth the new. How can we become rock solid to the point where we are not easily moved? We need to build a new sense of self stronger than you could have ever imagined. This is rare for you. Something no one would have thought you were capable of. You have been quiet long enough. Now is the time you shout out loud, so you can hear YOU.

Life isn't easy going all the damn time. Think of life as a roller coaster- up, down, down, up. Every individual is on a rollercoaster ride and I have felt the ups and downs of that ride throughout my ongoing existence. Life, I would say isn't pretty, but it sure is beautiful. I don't think it would be interesting without pain, regrets, or tough times.

I've opened new chapters and found myself closing squeaking doors to open the newly soundless door of light and knowledge, which is so warm and welcoming. There is definitely a connection amongst us all that's unseen and indestructible. When feeling alone, you are not. Somebody right now, this minute is going through exactly what you are going through. There are countless people in the world who have the same birthdates, same name, first and last- amazing how things work. Amazing how you made things work for you. Now is the time. Not yesterday. Yesterday will be a year ago eventually. You have handled it well, but are you ready to go again and really challenge yourself?

Making the most of every moment

Understanding we are one with slight differences

Unique stories can broaden our outlook about life

The following short stories are glimpses

Into the lives of people I've encountered

Based on their experiences

Written from my understanding and perception

Proceed with an open heart and mind

Reader discretion is advised

SANDRA'S LOST LEVEL 1

Some would look at me and prejudge. An overflowing bucket list of stereotypes before the grand gesture of a handshake and an identifiable name. Even if you knew my name, it still wouldn't spell pain. And what about my birth certificate? Ain't that 'spose to define the beginning of my bloodline? At least my Mother signed it. It said she was sixteen when she had me.

I always wondered about the blanked space where it said Father. From what I was told by my Aunt, my Mama's older sister, I wasn't his only child. So I'm wonderin' where in the world is my sister or brother. Do we favor each other? Same cheekbones, forehead, light brown eyes, would I ever know? My Mama was only nineteen when she moved to Chicago.

Some kids found her body in a neighborhood park. Beat, stabbed, and sodomized. That's in the words of my Aunt. Don't know what they relationship was like, I'm guessin' they wasn't that close. See, I'm thankful my Aunt took me in when my no good Mama abandoned me. She kept me fed, clothed, and I couldn't complain all that much, but how is a child 'spose to know what dysfunction looks like.

How you 'spose to know somethins' wrong when you wasn't taught that it wasn't. I was exposed to too much shit at a damn young age, and now that I look back, I can't stand they asses both. Goddamnit! Those muthafuckas. My Mama didn't have to open up all wide and let my deadbeat Daddy cum all up her vagina walls. Shit! See! This why I am the way I am today.

I miss my baby boy. He should be going on thirteen, fourteen, shit he could be fifteen for all I know. I stopped counting birthdays as bad as this shit sound. That Mexican bitch told me- wait, nope, yeah that's right it was that Black bitch. Not that Mexican bitch, but the Black bitch. The Black bitch said I was unfit, incapable, and unstable to take care of my baby.

Black old bitch! I'm the one who carried De'Andre for eight months and thirty days! Ha! That's nine months, hmm, I knew that. Damn. I needs me some more of this shit. I'm high as a god damn kite! Don't really feel like walking all the way down to Nikka's house for anotha though. Too damn far! Raining and shit! Colder than a well digger's booty in Montana outside.

Something ain't right... Thought that was the police outside my door, wait... Nah, that ain't them. I need a second opinion! Wish I had some company 'cus I'm feelin' sick. Laying on this floor, can't even cook them wangs I just got from that crowded ass grocery store! Shit, they probably spoiled by now. Been sittin' on that roach infested counter of mines for some days now.

I ain't got no appetite no way. Shit, I can't even think straight, huh, wonder why. My bestest friend , my little ol' besty, my fuckin' best friend sure is the devil. The devil and me hang all the damn time. Forty-one years old and look what I got to show, these raggedy ass pantyhose, cigarette burns in my couch cushions!

I DON'T GIVE A FAT FUCK! Black bitch said I couldn't have my son! (Sobbing) Said I couldn't have my son. I want 'em back! I'm tired, so tired. My bones ache, my back hurts, my hands are sore. How much could a bitch take? Jesus, oh Lord almighty Jesus! Jesus, show me the way. I know I ain't talked to you in a while, but damn I need help right now. Please help me, help me get my son back. I'm sick of this shit. I don't wanna cry no mo. Help, help me.

Reminder:

Recovery Awareness Level 1- Drowning: hopeless, despair, giving in, personal imprisonment, unbearable depression, lost, dead-ends, negative cycles consumes. Stress disguises as diseases, distortion, and destruction is prevalent.

Tip: Focus on becoming aware by answering reflection questions truthfully. Don't hold anything back. Don't filter yourself. Write down your answers if you would like to reference them later.

Reflection:

Sandra is stuck in a vicious cycle of destruction. While she may be hopeless and angry, she wants help to recover, help to get her son back. She needs to become aware addiction is all powerful. It doesn't stand aside just because you are a mother and have children you love, children you care for. It is a monster, pushing loved ones to the ground and pushing you into negativity every chance it gets. Be aware for when it pushes you down so you can stand right back up.

Who is Addiction pushing to the ground in your life?

Think of a time addiction pushed you into negativity, how did you react?

So, are you drowning or are you barely keeping your head above water?

Why are you in level 1 or do you remember a time you felt these feelings of level 1?

Write down some thoughts, feelings, and goals. Start with small goals that have the potential to help you get out of this near drowning level. Something as simple as telling a loved one you have an addiction to researching for resources such as meetings, therapists, or support groups. Even goals such as *finishing reading this book* will be a great start and help you become more aware. You don't have to do it all at once. Always remember to take one step at a time, one foot in front of the other.

LUIS AND LUST LEVEL 2

I thought having a baby girl would make me feel straight. I mean my senorita was like wifey material and every time we fucked, I could have gave her a son or two. Real talk, to be honest, I wasn't even in love with Mommy. Guess it was the food she made. I'm talking about bomb ass Menudo, almost better than Ma's.

If I needed new shirts, khakis, Jordans, Converse, she always, always had the money. Jose tatted both my arms, representin' where my pisas come from. We don't give a fuck. Beat you down bloody just for looking our way, like what's up homes. What, you didn't know? Nobody, I mean nobody fucked with us. Set 'em straight, one blow. POW!

Yeah, we stole, robbed. So what? Jose sold some weed and shit every now and then, kept so much dough in his pockets. One night, chillin' on the Eastside, our fuckin' rival gang came through bustin'. Jose pulled his piece from his belt and POP, POP! My first thought was to duck, but I ran like a little bitch. Running got me caught up.

Next thing I know, I'm in prison and the first visitor was Jose. He was pissed and the first thing he had said to me was, "You takin' care of Perra!" Then he spat on the glass separating me and him. He got away when he pulled triggers. I kept the code to the streets, but word got out in this new world I became involved in. I was somebody's little bitch. There I fucking said it! You ever been raped? I was. Tossed around like a Spaulding football to the next man, or should I say inmate 'cuz in prison you ain't a man. At least I wasn't.

Sat up counting days, thinking about my daughter wondering if she missed Daddy. Thought about killing myself. I was so close with a ripped sheet tied around my neck, but all I could think of was her.... My little Mija. Every guard, every fucking faggot I wanted to shank a thousand times. I replayed scenarios in my mind over and over again. My eyes were bloody red, filled with rage and shame. I hated myself. I hated myself for not being truthful with my baby Mama, my Ma, even Jose.

I came to a conclusion that I would never be the same again. Instead of working on the inside, I became obsessed with my physical shape. Biceps, triceps became my weapon. This time even crueler. I had no emotion on my release date, no money, no baby mama, no daughter. I spent six months in that after prison life shithole.

When I got back on the streets, I started making money the best way I knew how, sucked some dick, ate some food, fucked a nigga, got some weed, fucked this white nigga who lived lavish in a loft, he took care of me for a while. Unlimited clothes, anything I wanted. Sometimes I didn't have to ask. Unlimited supply of coke, weed, meth, then came that black tar. Fuck! Who gives a shit, my life is done anyway.

This became my new life and I honestly to be honest, didn't care. Anger controlled me. I was possessed, one glance in the mirror, and I snapped. Broken glass, bloody fist, and when he got home I snapped at him. Choked him 'till his pale skin turned purple. Then, then I let go. He kicked me out back on the street, but not before I stashed most of his jewelry.

I could barely chew the food the volunteers gave us homeless people. Three of my teeth were gone. Two on my right and one on my left. Not that I didn't expect it, I just wasn't used to this shit at the same time I still didn't care. One time I stole a handle of Vodka from Ralph's. I was too gone to even notice the protective seal it had on top.

When you want something you'd do anything to get it. I muscled with it and shattered the glass, bits of glass in Vodka didn't bother me, I just picked it out. Once my heart stopped, I was angry they brought me back to life. I laying there craving ice. That was the first thing on my mind. Not my daughter, I had given up. Too late. Daddy fucked up again.

Reminder:

Recovery Awareness Level 2- Head above water: exhaustion, dilemma, questioning, anger, high anxiety, insomnia, tension, caught in between fighting and giving up (swimming and sinking).

Reflection:

Luis is emitting anger in every which direction. The anger is geared to himself as he struggles with his identity and his addictions. He is questioning himself and he is in a dilemma of either being the father he wants for his daughter or giving up totally. Think of a time you faced a dilemma and began questioning yourself and your situation.

Are you currently facing a dilemma?

How did you feel and how did you react?

How can you allow reality to come into clear view and move to level 3?

The first step is awareness. Following awareness comes time for a decision/decisions. What do you want for yourself? How will you get there? What works for others may not necessarily work for you, but you have the internet, which has many blogs written by people who have been in your shoes and are in recovery. You have libraries stocked with books regarding not just how to recover from addiction, but facts about how addiction works and how it affects the body.

It is important to know the beast you are fighting, not just fighting alone is enough. You have therapists open to helping you and guiding you along the road to recovery. You have support groups, meetings, rehabs you can attend because you are not alone in this fight. The only way to know what works for you is to try one thing at a time and see for yourself.

KRISTIAN'S NIGHTMARE LEVEL 3

"*B*ut Dad, Jennifer's parents will be there, and I promise Dad, I promise I'll be home way before 12:30am."

Kristian stood in front of her father anticipating good news, which she was accustomed to receiving, eagerly waiting, tapping her spaghetti strapped sandal on the tile floor. Kristian stood five foot four, lips bright red covered with greasy gloss. Cover girl, Mac you name the brands; to her they were necessary even if she were out camping, which is something she would never even consider.

"Kris, last time..."

Before Kristian's father could finish his remark, his daughter rudely interrupted, flipping her dyed pink bobbed hair backwards.

"Daddy, that's in the past, and I can't believe you remember! That was seriously like two years ago. Dad, come on, Jennifer stays five exits away."

Kristian turns and faces the living room mirror mounted above the brick fireplace.

"Do I look okay?"

Kristian's father had been raising his daughter on his own since she was seven years old. He never got over his divorce since he was a man of his word and deeply meant every vow he had made to his ex-wife and losing her was more than devastating for him. However, when it came to Kristian, his heart became mush. He had an arduous time disappointing her. In his opinion, giving her too much freedom would make things much worse. Kristian would disrespect him without even thinking twice.

"Honey, everyday you look more and more like your mom." *Sigh* "Make sure you put gas in your car sweetheart and have Jennifer's parents contact me when you get there, okay? I have a caseload of work, so get home at a decent hour. I don't want to have to worry. Please don't make me worry"

Father O Father, seems like just yesterday. Do you remember when you gave me pecan ice cream? I sat on the swing, you stood behind me and gave me a huge push. I spilled that ice cream all over my Rug rats T-shirt. That was so funny. Gosh. I really miss those days. Oh, and Dad, remember that one amusement park, I think it could have been Disneyland. So many we went, I can't recall them all. I'm guessing my time away at college didn't sit too well with you.

  I have good news Dad. Dad, I said I have good news. Gosh, I hope these doctors are treating you well. Dad, I've never been through so much stress. Law school could never compare to how I'm feeling now, as I'm looking at you. Your skin looks so dry. How do I cope? How could you do this to me? I'm only twenty-eight, and all I wanted was for you to be proud of me.

  I can't possibly make this decision now! If only Mom... Dad, I wonder if... I wonder if you'd have traded all this in, you know? Putting me through school, my nice car, and countless shopping sprees. Even the beach house, the timeshares in Cancun, just to have Mom back. If she were here, you wouldn't be in this hospital. In this terrible coma. What did you do to yourself, Dad? I could have helped, you should have told me! This is how I find out! From my friend's mother! Yes, Dad, she had told me everything. Everyone in the neighborhood is talking about it.

  That's not the dad I remember, and you taught me better than that. It's sickening to think that you counseled clients while you were all choked up on that stuff. Gosh, I can hardly muster up the words to describe how I feel about this. To think this is the legacy I must follow. I will not, I will not be known as the daughter whose father's law firm... You know what Dad, I have to go, I love you, I'll see you sometime next week.

Reminder:

Recovery Awareness Level 3- Water to your chest: dismay, anticipation, reality comes in clear view.

Reflection:

    Kristian has just realized that her father is an addict. The Recovery Awareness Guidelines not only apply to addicts, but to anyone who has come into contact with someone who is an addict, whether that be a parent, son, daughter, friend, colleague, and so on. Perhaps you are reading this book because you have a loved one who is an addict or is in recovery. It is important to become aware of what is occurring and see everything for what it is, nothing more, nothing less. After becoming conscious, take to researching as mentioned before.

    Tools used by those in recovery can also be used by loved ones. There are specific support groups like Al-Anon. Make specific goals and try using these tools. Above all, believe. Believe in yourself and in your loved one's inner sober self. This story reveals addiction through the eyes of a loved one. Take this time to talk to your loved ones. Ask for support. Give support. Whether you are the addict or the loved one of an addict. What does support look like to you? Regardless of race, sex, class, education, we all need support on this road to recovery and in life. Once you become aware you are in level 3 and reality is staring back at you, reach out for support with open hands. Don't be afraid to ask for it. Don't be afraid to search for it.

NEFTWD AKA NEW ERA FOR THOSE WITH DISABILITIES

*T*hey pushed me into a locker today and at lunch they made fun of my lunch box and last Friday they called me names and that's when I ran to Mrs. Cullen's room, sat down at my desk crying. Mrs. Colleen gave me a fruit snack and that made me feel a lot better because I love fruit snacks. James hands them out when the bus drops all of my housemates off at home. I like our house and my room is bigger than the room I had at the "Cherished House".

The "Cherished House" sent me to NEFTWD- New Era For Those With Disabilities. They didn't give me fruit snacks there, they said that I behaved badly, but I said sorry when I pulled Monica's hair. I dunno know why I did it. Monica is my friend and we put the Nickelodeon puzzle pieces back together. I colored in my coloring book most of the time at the "Cherished House" and they never even took me on outings that much. One time everybody went to the zoo and me and my housemate Ryan stayed behind with Stacy to look after us. The other staff said we would be too much trouble. I woulda behaved.

They think I'm stupid, but I understand a lot. I know one thing, I'm not stupid. Every Tuesday and Thursday I go and see my speech therapist. His name is Dr. Stevens, I've been with him for four years, and he really likes my jokes. I even have a folder full of jokes that James gave me. Dr. Stevens thinks I'm silly. When James picked me up yesterday, Dr. Stevens said that I should perform in front of my housemates. James smiled and said that we could make it happen.

Now I'm really happy, but sometimes I get real sad, sometimes angry when it's just my grandma visiting me. She tells me I was a miracle baby and that my Mom is doing okay in treatment. I don't know what she means by that. I think she has asthma like me because I get treatments too, twice a day at NEFTWD. Ryan scares me a lot, he never participates in our inclusion activities. Plus he laughs when he pokes me. I wish he would stop doing that.

I told my house manager James about it, now Ryan has to wash dishes forever! I vacuum all five bedroom, and the staff lets me play Michael Jackson while I clean up. I love the Thriller song. James puts it on repeat for me. After my chores, I help take out food items for dinner. Tonight we are having my favorite- cheesy lasagna, salad, tons of tomatoes, garlic bread, yum! After we eat, it's my housemate Tanya's turn to choose what movie we get to watch. I'm hoping she picks Back To The Future, or Ironman, but she'll probably pick Princess Diaries like she always does.

NEFTWD FOLLOW UP

Alcohol beverages have warning labels mentioning its harmful effects. It says that pregnant women should not drink alcohol. Alcohol consumption during one's pregnancy can cause FAS, Fetal Alcohol Syndrome. Children born with FAS usually have growth deficiencies, scoliosis, cleft lips, physical, and cognitive defects. They may have trouble understanding wrong from right. Consumption of alcohol in the third trimester can lead to postnatal growth retardation. Similar effects are high risk for children whose mothers either smoked marijuana or took drugs during their pregnancies. Even cigarettes can have serious complications.

I have worked in group homes and programs for the developmental disabilities population in the past. I must say, group homes and programs are nothing like they seem from the outside looking in. It's absolutely disturbing how some people that work in this field could care less about the developmental disabilities population. Some are in the field just to earn a paycheck.

A woman I had worked with would rather talk about what she did and where she went for her weekend to other employees instead of tending to her client and responsibilities. From her actions, her client ended up drinking bleach that she had left unattended. She gave him milk and did not think to call the poison control. So I called and the next day she was terminated.

In Pasadena, California, a program called E. Villa Esperanza Services terminated me for speaking up to the local regional center representative when they conducted an annual audit. There were more than forty clients in one rented hall, with below average conditions. When it was hot, the air conditioning didn't work. When it was cold, the heat wouldn't come on. Instructors had clients coloring, drawing, painting fingernails for longer than other activities that could have been more beneficial for their improvement.

I told the regional center representative the point blank truth- this place is nothing like it is when you are here during the inspection. I could not believe how my co-workers put on such a show and made something so dirty look so squeaky clean. Within a week I was called to the office across from the rented hall. I was greeted by my manager and her supervisor. They fired me. My client's mother could not believe the news when I told her. She actually had a gut feeling about their negligence. This is a touchy subject. I suggest to anyone who has a child, relative, or friend in programs/group homes to be cautious and to look under the surface. Not everything is what it seems.

FADED DREAMS LEVEL 1

*L*ooking from the outside in, you'd think this glamour is all that life is about. Perfection lingers around like the scent from a woman that just left from my Ritz Suite on the fifteenth floor. It's pretty tough when you're engaged and your life takes unexpected detours. You're the center of attention in public, and I can't remember the life I led before my big break. It's going on eight years since I went back home to Denver.

My finances are scarce and all these public appearances are driving me crazy, not to mention these younger actors are getting all the roles I should be receiving. My mind is going a mile a minute and my fucking agent sets me up to do this public service announcement. I could barely remember the script that they sent me and when I got to the studio they changed most of it, if not all of it.

Then came the teleprompter, which I could hardly read. Alcohol reeked in my trailer moments beforehand. I had received a phone call from my fiancée Joan, screaming and crying about accusations from media sources. It's all true, but what am I supposed to tell her? No way, I just couldn't hurt her. At times I do feel I should call off our engagement, but then I'd be alone again.

I said I would do this PSA sober, but that's impossible now. My assistant's telling me to straighten up, when he is the one who just brought these IPAs in. The network didn't even consider using the PSA, so I didn't get a check. It was a complete waste of my fuckin' time. My buddy's having a video shoot in San Fernando Valley, think I'll drop by. Last party he threw had massive hot babes and massive blow.

I ended up by the outdoor pool in my underwear. I haven't slept and all the platters of food just make me nauseous. All I want is some massive blow. Now I'm anxious and fuckin' frustrated. My life is a nightmare; my face is growing peach fuzz. I'm losing it, can't get a grip. I would pay a hitman to end my existence. Have him put the barrel to my tonsils and tell him to squeeze as hard as he can. Maybe I'll do it myself.

Reminder:

Recovery Awareness Level 1- Drowning: hopeless, despair, giving in, personal imprisonment, unbearable depression, lost, dead-ends, negative cycles consumes. Stress disguises as diseases and distortion. Destruction is prevalent.

Reflection:

The addict has hit rock bottom. He no longer can perform his job, he is frustrated, and he feels like there is no way out of addiction. Use this time to become aware of these level 1 feelings and signs you may have experienced in the past, or are currently experiencing. What can you do to help yourself? What has worked in the past? What has not worked? It is extremely important to learn from your experiences and stop the negative cycles.

How can you use this awareness as a tool during not only recovery but in your life overall? A great way to get started is keeping a journal. Now, you don't have to write in it everyday but take time out of your busy day to write a couple sentences, which may soon become paragraphs, and even pages. Allow yourself to feel and understand what is going on inside and around you. To take it one step further, write to yourself. What would you say to yourself? What advice do you have for yourself? Sometimes, it is easy to give others advice that you should be listening to yourself.

Start believing in YOU

ONLY ON SPECIAL OCCASIONS LEVEL 2

"*I*'ve tried and she won't listen. Yes, I understand she's my sister, but that doesn't justify her actions. This is supposed to be my special day with my special someone. If she can't get her act together, I might just put her on the back burner for a while. I mean, didn't you see her at Travis' wedding? Not to mention George's gathering after his big football game win.

Mom, listen, she's the reason our little brother was so embarrassed in front of his friends. Mom, Tracy needs to change. I'm not sure if I want her at my wedding. She ruins everything and never shows any remorse. How *disrespectful can someone be? Mom, I don't believe that. Every sentence that comes out of Tracy's mouth is just one huge lie. She wasn't at her therapist's office. How do I know that? Mom, come on, she stopped by my work at 2:00 pm.*

She looked worn and frankly I am fed up with her surprises. It makes me look really bad, Mom. Mom, I didn't mean to make you cry. Mom, don't cry please. Gee, No, I'm not saying to give up on her. What does Dad think about all this? Mom, Dad needs to stop. She spends all that money on alcohol and who knows what. Mom, I'm just being honest. Tracy just sweet talks her way in with Dad. No, I'm not giving her a hard time, she is giving you and Dad a real hard time.

You have to let her grow up. George needs you too. He can't see his parents stressed all the time because his aunt is a raging alcoholic. Sorry Mom, it's just that Tracy gets under my skin. I need to talk to Tracy? Ha. What for? Oh, to tell her she's not welcomed at my wedding, and my reception, my job, and my home. If that makes you happy then I'll call her now, Mom. I'm sorry for my rant. Mom, I love you so much. Tell Dad and George I say hello."

Tina hangs up the phone, goes through her contacts, and dials Tracy's number. Tracy answers in a dazed and drowsy tone.

"What do you want Tina, I'm busy. Oh fuck...Shucks!"

Tina rolls her eyes.

"What are you doing over there? Never mind that. I don't want to know."

Tracy starts to wipe her table off.

"No, no, no, no, no. I'll tell you what I'm fucking doing Tina. You fuckin' made me spill almost half of my Sauvignon Blanc!"

"Tracy, I thought you didn't drink wine."

Tracy tosses her cleaning cloth on her burgundy rug.

"Honey, I drink everything. This is actually Vodka. I just wanted to sound sophisticated like my little sister, ha ha. What do you want from me Tina? Company's coming and I haven't showered... I smell like you right now... Like a dog."

Tina's jaw drops in a state of shock.

"Are you insinuating that I'm a bitch?"

"What do you think, Tina?"

"Tracy, don't answer a question with a question."

"Well, you never answered my question. What is it that you want from me, Tina? Money? No couldn't be that. You have that already. I forgot for a second there, princess bitch."

"Oh my God, Tracy. What has gotten into you? You're drunk right now aren't you? Aren't you?"

"Well, doesn't that happen when the glass gets empty? Come on Tina. I'm celebrating."

"Celebrating for what, Tracy?"

"Do you have a glass? Raise your glass, I want. Uh. Um. I want." (belch)

"I want to make a toast. Cheers to my little know it all, skinny sister! Come on Tina, this is a once in a lifetime deal!"

"Deal? What are you talking about? My God you're sick! This is exactly why I did not want to call you. Please stop. Do not come by my work. It's embarrassing!"

"I don't care. I don't care. I don't fuckin' care. I only drink on special occasions. Why don't you lose my number. I'll celebrate again when you stop calling ME... Bitch."

Reminder:

Recovery Awareness Level 2- Head above water: exhaustion, dilemma, questioning, anger, high anxiety, insomnia, tension, caught in between fighting and giving up (swimming and sinking).

Reflection:

     Both Tina and Tracy are experiencing level 2 in their own ways. It seems as though they are very angry with one another, but if you look closer it isn't personal, they are angry because of Tracy's alcoholism. It is very important that when you experience an emotion and become aware of it, that you look deep inside for the source.

     For example, have you ever yelled at someone only to later realize that you were angry because of something that happened last week, maybe even last month, or last year? The next time you experience an intense emotion, instead of reacting, respond. Take a deep breath, become aware of your body, and respond. This is not an easy process, but over time it becomes second nature with practice and patience.

NEEDLE IN A HAYSTACK LEVEL 3

"*I don't have to answer to no one. I go and leave as I please. So what? I don't care. What?! You don't want me by your store!*"

Tasha was known to cause mayhem in her neighborhood, raised eyebrows, and honking horns from men as she'd strut her petite body down street corners. She started her day by standing some feet away from the Lee's Liquor store. Pedestrians on their i-Phones would drop change in Tasha's fountain drink cup that she got from McDonald's. The owner of Lee's Liquor became agitated as she would disturb his customers as they left from his store.

He tried to get her to leave, but she would cause a scene and react aggressively, kicking meaningless items off the sidewalk, screaming.

Lee's Liquor store owner shouts out to Tasha

"No! You go now. I call police. They come get you! You not wanted here. You owe me. You owe me dollar and fifty cent. Yes! You owe, you owe me!"

A customer walks out of Lee's Liquor and drops change in Tasha's fountain drink cup.

"No! Don't give her money. You give to me!"

The customer shrugs her shoulders, opens up her Nature Bar, and continues on her way.

Tasha responds, yelling loudly

"Fuck you Lee. I do what I want! Call the boys in blue! I'm leaving anyhow. Your customers are full of shit, just like you, Lee! Cheep like you, Lee!!! I don't owe you a damn penny!"

Lee grabs his broom and begins to sweep the cigarette butts away from the store's entrance.

"No you cheap! Next time I call police. They come get you!"

Tasha picks up a cigarette from the ground with only a couple centimeters left of tobacco, walks away, and turns down a quiet street occupied with working women and transgender individuals.

"Dammit! Why do they have to be here when I show up? I'm glad I had this outfit to wear. Ohhh, I love her shoes. They would look better on me though. That bitch took my trick last week and had the audacity to even flaunt the money she made in front of me. I'm not even going to say hi to that hoe. Selfish tramp! I shared the last of my Crystal with that skank. Here comes somebody right now. Let me show her how it's done."

A silver Audi pulls up to the curb. The driver rolls the window down, Tasha walks up and leans against the door, sticking her head inside the window space.

"Hey babe, nice car. Look even better if I was in it, don't you think?

The man smiles, and turns his radio notches down.

"Yeah, a lot could be better. Better if you were with me somewhere and I was in you. Why don't you hop in. I have an hour or so to spare before I head back to work."

"Okay, babe."

Tasha opens the passenger door and takes a seat. The driver rests his hands on her thigh and asks.

"How much for a blow job, hun?"

She points at her private area and then grabs the driver's hand.

"Go ahead. Touch it. Wait, show me money first. I'll charge eighty for the whole thing."

The driver retracts his hand and reaches in his pockets for cash.

"I only have forty right now. I forgot to go to the ATM. Sex next time. BJ works for me right now. I only have an hour or so. I still have to drop off my wife's lunch before I head back to work. Close your door, I'll find somewhere else to park."

Tasha accepted the forty dollars and takes off to find her dealer.

"Well, that was a quick one. I know this time I won't be sharing any of my shit with those hoes down there. I have the most clientele anyway. Flat asses even had the nerve to talk about my breakouts on my face, but look who has the goods now and who wouldn't want this? At least I still have some meat left on my bones. So what I'm a druggie and a whore? At least I support myself. Ain't nothin' wrong with that".

Reminder:

Recovery Awareness Level 3- Water to your chest: dismay, anticipation, reality comes in clear view.

Reflection:

Tasha has a very clear view of her surroundings and actions, but what she is missing is the awareness for the need for change. Not just change as in quarters and dimes, but true life change. Change can be scary.

What do you think is holding Tasha back from wanting change or from being aware that she needs change?

What do you think is holding you back or what held you back in the past?

There are things in our lives we can not change and it is important to accept what we can not change. However, one of the things we can work on changing every day is our behavior. We definitely can't change the past. We can't change other people, but we can change ourselves. Make a list of behaviors (addiction and non-addiction related) you would like to work on changing or improving. Next to each item, make a plan on how you would like to change these behaviors or what tools you will use to make these changes. This will help you move on to the next levels of awareness and allow you to realize you are in control. You are improving!

*If you're thinking about change
Chances are you are on the right track*

THE SUPPLIER
LEVEL 4

"**H**ow you think I pay my bills? Ain't nobody hiring a felon. My stomach growls just like yours. How you think I put gas in my car? How you think I got these new shoes and them clean rims? I do what I have to do to survive in these streets. I got three baby mamas and all my babies need diapers and shit. Today was a good day. I made at least a hundred more than last night. That's 'cuz I got that good-good. That fire! What you need? I got them pills too. Norco, Vicodin.

    Got that syrup. Got that soft. Got that hard. That Mama Coca, Happy Dust, Sweet Hardball, that Aunt Hazel. You know that China White. Eighths of that Mother Mary. Even got something to speed you up, or slow you down so you can relax and go to sleep. I'm the doctor. Fuck with me. Leave them young fools alone selling that no good, bull, garbage. If you ain't from 'round here, my shit'll let you know you fuckin' with the real.

I got shit that'll keep ya dick up for three days, boy! Gotta watch my back 24/7. Some fools start trippin' and get jealous when they see how good you doing. Shit. Just last weekend they shot up my block and I heard they were looking for one of my patnas that owed them some weight. That's why I don't borrow shit from nobody. If I ain't got it, then I ain't got it. I ain't tryna get caught up over some bullshit.

I make sure I got my mini-me with me for protection. Just in case. 'Cause if they start shootin' at me, I'ma fire back and make sure I blow a muthafucka head off. Don't play with my life. Like I said I got some diapers to buy and mouths to feed. It ain't like I stand up here all day for fun and amusement! You get tired of these fiends tryna get a little extra. Talking 'bout they gone bring you some movies. Ten minutes later, the damn fiend come back with VHS tapes of Lion King and Secrete Garden.

Muthafucka that ain't gone get you higher. I take cash, not no ancient ass VHS tapes of Mufasa. I thought they stopped making VCRs in the first place. I see the fiend kids and they don't realize I'm most likely the reason why they ain't got no school clothes. Fuck it, that's all I can say. Gotta worry 'bout mines. Shit we all got problems. Maybe I'd feel different if this wasn't all I knew. If I didn't get my bitch pregnant and had never did that robbery, I could be somewhere in Vegas sippin' Ciroc with my pinkie up. You feel me?

That ain't gonna happen though. Gotta deal with the law. The system got me all fucked up. I'm right where they want me to be. Like a fucking puppet. Controlled. Fuck the damn judge. That judge could never walk a minute in my Lugs. Telling a grown man to stay out of trouble. You ain't my daddy nigga! I ain't no little ass kid. If anything, I'm in some drama. Drama every damn day where I'm making my rent money. Bitches slappin' bitches. Baby mamas slashin' tires and breakin' fools windows.

It's rough. I don't know when I'ma make it out. It's the same shit every day. Same cars, same faces, same barber. Same hiding spaces where I stash my shit. I don't let that shit show, how I'm feelin' inside and shit. I try to not let it bother me. Three sons I got three sons. I be damned if they live life like their pops, but their mama's got them on a tight grip. I just worry about them calling their step daddy, daddy. That would fuck me up.

I'ma get my shit straight, hopefully. Get a nice spot out here with a pool, teach my sons how to swim, make sure they go to school and treat a bitch right, and teach them how to drive a stickshift. Shit like that they will remember. I didn't have a daddy, never met him. I don't know if he dead or alive. He had my mama struggling with five kids all on her own.

Only dad I had was Big Unc on the block. Taught me how to cook crack, weigh weed, and bag it. I thought he was GOD growing up. Shinning so bright with his jewels. He always had a bunch of bitches with him. He told me that there's two ways to live your life, dignified or lost in sorrow. Think I need to work on having dignity. Big Unc got shot up coming from some Gentleman's Club. I couldn't believe it. I'm trying to make it out of here. I'm not ready to be in Heaven yet. Gotta right my wrongs."

Reminder:

Recovery Awareness Level 4- Water to your waist: risking, spontaneous, fluid, inspired, energetic, focused, fearful.

Reflection:
Unlike Tasha from the previous story, the supplier is not only aware of everything going on around him, he is aware that he needs to change his behaviors and his lifestyle, which lands him in level 4. He specifically finds inspiration for change in his daughter and in the tragedy that happened to his father figure.

Where do you find your inspiration? It doesn't have to be a person, although most of the time it includes our loved ones. It could be being a part of nature and being a tiny piece of something so amazing and gigantic! It could be a talent of yours such as singing, drawing, painting, cooking, etc. It can be anything and everything you want it to be. Create a list of your inspirations and put it up where you can see it every day, first thing in the morning. Use it to power yourself up.

FLOAT FORWARD LEVEL 5

A soft breeze lifts me up
Drops me off into a clear river
Pebbles, rocks, earth below me
Bright, free, careless
I begin to float forward
Leaving behind a wall of red sequoias
I take with me a handful of opportunities,
A destination unknown to me,
And time
Twisting, turning
Strength holds me up
As I float forward
Wishing, hoping
Regrets slide off entwined branches
Open to possibilities
The sun and moon each lend an ear
I am happy

> I am healthy
> I am safe
> I am loved
> I am abundant
> I am peace
> I am compassion
> I am fearless
> I am greatness
> I am powerful
> I am in gratitude
> The breeze that once carried me
> Grabs hold of my words
> Carries them off
> As I continue to float forward

Reminder:

Recovery Awareness Level 5- Water to your feet: relaxed, settled, accomplished, self-aware, loving oneself, opening heart, freedom, purity, cleansed, able to love, awake, peace, contentment, reasoning, clarification, evolved, elation.

Reflection:
    What has sobriety, clarity, freedom, and accomplishment looked like for you in the past? What does it look like currently if you are experiencing it now? What do you imagine it will look like? What do you hope it will look like? Close your eyes and visualize it. You are there in that moment. What do you see, smell, hear, feel, touch?

    Once you complete the visualization, write an affirmation like the one in the poem above. Begin each sentence with I am and complete it with what you felt as a result of your visualization. You can say this affirmation every morning, or evening or just when you need it. Now celebrate and keep doing what it is that is working for you! This is your journey, embrace it.

FACTS

It's unfortunate how we lose innocent people due to someone's irrational deportment. For instance, in 2012 over 10,000 people died in drunk driving crashes. The fatalities were slightly lower in the previous year of 2011; which was 9,865 according to the National Highway Traffic Safety Administration.[1] Those individuals could have been someone's mother, father, wife, husband, daughter, or son. Someone you could have known personally. They could have been students who were hoping for a better chance at life once finished with college. However, to the world they will be known as a statistical number or faces of a billboard as a reminder of what could happen when someone decides to get behind the wheel intoxicated.

An acquaintance of mine drives a pocket-sized hellish red Volvo. One contrite night after dancing and having a good time, we had gotten into his teeny Volvo despite the fact he was inebriated. He had driven on the freeway, speeding while slightly swerving in and out the adjacent lanes. Surely, we could have easily hit someone. I was unaware of how many damn drinks he had before this ordeal. If we were to crash that would have been it for us. His Volvo was not in too good of shape, not to mention his seat belts were not functioning at a considerable level. Alcohol mixed with his childlike parade was enough for me never to ride shotgun ever again with him.

Concerned citizens have merged together to develop awareness through numerous organizations like Students Against Destructive Decisions and Mothers Against Drunk Driving. Alcohol can produce death and has produced death. The Centers For Disease Control and Prevention reported that about 30 people per day in the US die in car crashes involving a drunk driver, which is about 1 death every 51 minutes.[2] These are deaths that can be prevented. Finally, on average, a drunk driver has driven under the influence 80 times before their first arrest![3] These statistics are frightening and it is important to be aware of the facts.

Cocaine and crack, derived from the coca leaf that's found in Southern America, is the second most trafficked illegal drug in the world. Repeated use can cause cerebral hemorrhage, heart attack, respiratory failure, and other harmful effects, according to the Drug Free World Organization. Cocaine also lowers one's inhibitions and causes aggressive behaviors amongst its users. Stroke and seizures are common fatalities when using cocaine. In 2006, a survey supervised by the National Survey on Drug Use and Health reported that 35.3 million Americans over the age of 12 reported having used cocaine.[4]

In many circumstances, users were infected with HIV from infectious needles carrying the virus. This hits home for me since my mother's mother died from AIDS; her partner was an avid drug user. We have heard about the late 1970s and early 1980s rise of crack that infiltrated communities. That history is still vibrant and very much so present to this day in ghettos across the United States.

Crack sells rampantly in city streets. Where this takes place, it's usually the norm to know the drug dealers. Some stand on corners for hours until they meet their quota. For some, that will be the only life that they know. For instance, this guy I knew for several months would only talk about his "block" and how that was the only place where he felt comfortable because he knew all the fellas who'd stand around smoking weed, drinking malt liquor, talking about everyone who walked by, calling women bitches all in front of operating businesses on this busy sidewalk.

One day I took him out of his element and his insecurities about himself were revealed through his outrageous negative outbursts regarding everyone he saw. Not everyone is flexible, but I couldn't understand how someone could be so accustomed to doing the same things every day and not have some sort of wake up call. He hinted constantly on the fact that he wanted to go back to the "block". From his whining, we never made it to the pool hall. Honestly, you can't blame the man. This is what he was raised into, shielded from possibilities, but I know deep down inside of him he has a positive passion for something. My only hope is that he eventually finds his way. Although this man is in his late 40s, it's never too late to have a mental shift.

Speaking of mental, alcohol can damage brain cells and nerve cells. When blood alcohol levels are extremely high, the central nervous system slows down, which in turn may cause cardiac failure and comas. The longer it's used, the more likely you could have intestinal bleeding and ulcers. My father suffered the dread of ulcers, which was devastating for me to hear. Pain is not only experienced by the abuser but is also inflicted among loved ones who are seeing someone they care about deteriorating.

I definitely did not deal with my father's addiction in a healthy way. Subconsciously, I numbed the pain through the cycle I had been completing. I made myself not feel for years and ignored all emotions until they spilled over, showing up in unrelated situations throughout my life. However, I have come to a conclusion that time is forever changing and you are not getting any younger. What are you waiting for? Really ask yourself and seep into that question. Have you really challenged yourself?

Okay, maybe you are waiting for your problems to go away. Well, guess what, problems and difficulties are a part of life. Be brave enough to tackle all obstacles on impact, just as soon as they arrive. Notice what the issues are. Do not dwell. The more you think about these problems, the more these problems will sway you back to the uncomfortable cold and darkness. Nothing positive is changing when you are constantly dwelling. You will be creating stress and making small problems into a mountaintop full of problems. Do not ignore and pretend that these problems are not there. You will have a battle with your inner voice nagging you. Come up with concrete solutions, a game plan and then execute it! You will be able to move forward with a clean conscious.

I have been there with overwhelming amounts of problems, choosing the wrong path instead of finding a solution. My rent was due and I was on the verge of being evicted. I ignored the issue and drank heavily until I received the final notice. I should have been sober and brave enough to tackle the problem head on. I could have come up with a solution, but I dwelled in panic and stress. I realized that you have to be ready for anything to happen, nowadays. Fluently prepare for the good and the ugly. Previous attempts of the same method did not work. It is time to look at things differently and tackle those problems with a fresh approach. Focus on the positive.

Yes, you have fucked up so many times and suffered the repercussions, but now let's give that deflating negative a rest. What about all the great things you have done? What about the great things you aspire to achieve? Focus on this and the more attention given, the more likely great things will continue to happen for you. It is time to be a winner now! You might have lost your job a while back because of a random drug test, but that woke you up to become a better and responsible individual. You still have options! It's not the end of the world.

Look at it this way; sometimes things happen in order for you to grow and to be put back on track. It may be hard to see at the time, but the universe is working with you, aligning your life in the right place. I have learned to go with the flow and ride this life's ride however long possible. Having faith that everything will turn out perfectly fine goes a long way. Some people may think that is not a realistic notion, but from my experience, it has brought me far and wide. Life can get dull and uninteresting living life like a robot; programmed and what have you. This is your life!

If you really, deep down inside, want to get better, have unwavering faith that no matter what, you will get better. No one else is walking in your shoes. Your situation is unique, just like your character. Your outcome is completely different than my outcome. At the same time, we are very similar. Our journeys may be different, which is why we can learn from their stories, my story, in order to create our story. We have struggled to hold on tightly gripping sanity. We have felt pain that most could never understand or relate with. For that is a gift to be able to share your struggle in hopes of opening doors for others.

SOURCES

1. "Impaired Driving." *Impaired Driving.* National Highway Traffic Safety Administration, n.d. Web. 17 July 2015. <http://www.nhtsa.gov/Impaired>.

2. Impaired Driving: Get the Facts." *Centers for Disease Control and Prevention.* Centers for Disease Control and Prevention, 19 May 2015. Web. 17 July 2015.<http://www.cdc.gov/motorvehiclesafety/impaired_driving/impaireddrv_factsheet.html>.

3. "Drunk Driving Statistics." *MADD.* N.p., n.d. Web. 17 July 2015. <http://www.madd.org/drunk-driving/about/drunk-driving- statistics.html>.

4. "International Statistics." Drug Free World. N.p., n.d. Web. 17 July 2015. <http://www.drugfreeworld.org/drugfacts/cocaine/international-statistics.html>.

IN A NEW LIGHT

Mist in air
Mid morning dew
Fog fades
Wind sings lyrics
Birds chirp along in tune
Debris fills city streets where city sleeps
All this is in between
Why I read and write in between lines and rhyme schemes
Moment of life just intensified
Why haven't we or I seen this before in real time?
Where emotions exist & a tear should drop as you read this
Pain floods blocks leaving trails of despair,
Regrets and those how did I get heres
Once upon a time these stories were passed down differently
Or some chapter went missing
Which lead to this outcome
How come it was that discreet
Hidden beneath soil and skeletal bones
Timidly collapsing
Nonresponsive
Nonreactive
Too numb to know what love felt like anymore

Neglected dreams rodent to marijuana leafs
Illegally consuming the best thing since ice cream
At least that's what was told to me
Not verbally
Cravings tremendously strong
They spoke to me
Through eyes
Like reading poetry

MY BEGINNINGS

I was seven years old when I first experienced inebriation. I recall that fraction of my childhood being quite devious. This took place in San Diego and in our apartment complex in Linda Vista. My oldest brother had just been released from prison and my family held a drunken celebration for him. Although it was not my mother's intentions for her last born to get fucked up, it happened anyway. In my make believe wonderland, I was the waitress serving margaritas to my siblings, and my mom was the lazy bartender behind the bar getting drunk herself.

Why does that humongous punch cup make so much noise? I wondered, is that a slushy she's pouring in that cup? Inquisitive, I was and wanted a say so on how good it must have tasted since my mother smacked her lips after sipping it. My mom would open the freezer, pull out the arctic ice cubes, and place them in the humongous loud punch making machine. As I got older, I sure did know how to work a blender from K-mart- the name brand ones. She would then say, "here, give this to your brother." When she was done adding all the magical potions, I would look at her and wrinkle my eyebrows so that they would move up and down in sequence as I twirled my tiny fingers in deviance.

"All done mama, all done?"

My mother cursed like a sailor and her all time favorite word was "Shit!" followed by "Goddammit, shit!" When she was stressed about life, she'd be sitting on the toilet, talking to herself about problems while taking a shit, at the same time drinking a thirty-two ounce Miller High Life. Finally, my patience paid off and she passed me this magical potion. I walked away nice and slowly, vacated her presence, turned the corner, took a quick swat team look down the staircase, and saw my brother, my sister, and my eldest brother. Okay, think of something I thought as I turned to point A with my back against the wall.

I took five steps sideways to the left, saw my mom, and then took five steps sideways back to point A. Thinking, should I do it? I nodded my head, yes I should. Slowly I put the cup to my lips, tilt, gulp, and holy cow this is really good! I then took two, three, four, five, six more gulps. Finally, I turned back to the staircase and walked down like the waitress I would soon seem to be. I stood there directly in front of my brother and said "Here you go. Mama said to bring it to you"

Then my sister exclaims, "What!? Bring me one too!" That's how it all started. I handled a few more runs and by that time I was already on my fifteenth gulp. Boy, oh boy did they start to notice. After walking up and down those stairs, they started to look closer than I had realized; I tumbled dry.

"Dang, what's wrong with her," my sister asked concernedly to everyone downstairs. "She seems a little um... different." My sister is five years older than me, but she acted older than that. Can you scream boys! I would follow her around outside of our apartment complex, focused on each of my footsteps, careful not to make a sound, I was quite as a mouse.

My brother turned toward me while raising his margarita cup, "did you drink some of this?" He was the type of brother who would act caringly, but not give a damn about a damn thing. For instance, back when we lived in ghetto West Oakland, he murdered our house cat Tiger and let him rot in a black hefty garbage bag, or so I was told, but the legend is actually true whether you believe it or not.

He would even beat up my other brother who was five years younger than him, just for watching television. I heard that from the source. Even though my eldest brother was related by blood, that connection which was never there turned into dislike, which to my understanding, he never was a brother to me anyway. Now my second eldest brother or should I just say my big bro, always looked out for me even when I rolled around in the grass at seven while intoxicated.

"Umm," as I tried to stand up straight like the statue of liberty, which failed horribly. In a split second. I heard timber! WHAM!

"Mama! She been drankin'!" My brother yelled as if to tattle tale.

Then my sister whispered in my ear, "ohhhh, he 'bout to tell on you." It all happened in moment's time; my eldest brother jotted upstairs while skipping a few and spilling the last of his margarita.

"Mama, you know she been drinkin' this whole time, she downstairs fallin'. First, she was standin' up, but she started swayin' like she ain't got no sense." My mother could hardly hear too well and I could tell she was a bit fixed from her drinks.

From upstairs, I suddenly heard, "Huh? What you say now, huh? What you say? Shit. Where my cigarettes? You been smoking my damn cigarettes? Shit. Cigarettes cost five dollars!"

"Mama, I said she downstairs drunk, how we gonna go out to eat still?

"She downstairs drunk? Shit, we still gonna go out to eat, how she get drunk? Y'all got my baby drunk? Goddammit shit!" Minutes later my mother came downstairs with GPS in one hand and her margarita in the other. For as long as I could remember, she smoked except for three years when I was a teenager.

"You been drinkin', huh? How you get drunk, shit! How you get drunk?" I could tell she wasn't expecting an answer, as she would always speak around sentences and grasp onto other subjects. "Where my keys at, shit. I'm ready to go eat, I'm hungry!"

My sister grabbed her keys from the coffee table, "Here you go mama."

"Come on! Y'all ready? Y'all gone give me a heart attack running up in here like that. Oh me oh my what y'all gonna do when I die?"

My sister had turned away and then turned back facing our mother, "Mama why you gotta say stuff like that?"

My mother put her hand on her hip, rattling her car keys in the other, and shouted, "Don't worry 'bout it. Come on! Go on, I'm hungry. Where ya other brother at? He bet not be with that boy from… Where the hell he from anyway? That's why I don't like him, don't know shit about him. He just a bad influence, I can't stand that little boy. Why y'all still standin' 'round, come on, I said let's go, shit. Ohh, y'all just drive me crazy."

This could have been on average an everyday episode of loud voices, hollering from one room to the next. Years slowly passed and I had developed an inner struggle. I did not know what the future had in store for me, but I would soon realize how substance abuse would affect me.

LA EXPERIENCE

How did I end up on the greyhound bus? I had awakened up to silence and behold there were three shots of liquor in my grey hoodie pocket. I sat in the second row, gazed out the window to my left. Highway five going south, views of mountains brought me into deep wandering thoughts. Where am I going? What am I doing? I decided that there wasn't any point of my questioning. I wasn't even halfway there yet so I took a swig, closed my eyes and fell back into my dreamlike trance.

Life could not have been any more stressful. I was living in Antioch, California which is a small city forty-five minutes from Berkeley. The times were behind there, and most of the time I felt out of place and foreign. Meth addicts roamed in parking lots. There were desolate bars; some bars were so far away hidden down on unlit roads. It was almost like they could have been the plot line of some murderous serial killer film. I was accustomed to a faster lifestyle, so living there depleted me of my dreams, and conjured up lost feelings of depression. I was constantly reminded that I was grown and unwanted at mom's house.

Although she was right, she confused me so much that I was uncertain about my life. She would tell me to get out and then the next minute she'll tell me to stay. Other times she would make random suggestions like the time she told me to have a baby to receive large amounts of government assistance. I never knew what the next foul statement my mother would come up with.

I had no idea where I was when I got off the bus. I wouldn't say lost because I didn't feel lost. I remembered a resource number a friend had told me about. The famous 211! There I was, suitcase on wheels, huge black backpack, walking down an unfamiliar street, dripping with chunks of sweat. I hadn't realized how many more degrees hotter it would be in Southern California.

It was apparent that I stood out like a sore thumb or a blazing red pimple. I had to take a break and regain my wind and by that I mean gather my thoughts and perhaps smoke a cigarette. I had been craving one since that long ass ride from the Bay Area to Los Angeles! I lit one despite the fact I could barely breathe to begin with from the walking I was doing, not to mention that heavy backpack I was tagging along with. I was in "Go Gadget Go" mode and not one thing could stop me, not even my lungs. I had a sense of determination that I would find food and shelter by any means necessary. Okay, time for business, I whipped my cell phone out of my pocket and start dialing the 211 number.

"211. How may I help you?"

The operator must have been having a lovely day, or maybe too much coffee. I was taken aback at his enthusiasm.

"Yes, Hi. I'm homeless, and I need a place to stay."

"Mam, I can help you with resources, please state your name and zip code."

Fucking zip code!

"Uhh, I don't know the zip code, sir."

"Do you have a source of income?"

"No."

The operator lowered his tone of voice, "I need your zip code so I can help you out a little better, mam."

He sounded older, so I called him sir, but him calling me mam was so displeasing. I had drifted some long graphitized blocks away from the Greyhound station. To my displeasure, I had to go back, otherwise, I would not be able to get this help that I was anxious to receive. I just wished I had thought about this call before I ended up on some street I couldn't pronounce. There weren't even any people walking on the sidewalks that I could ask for the zip code. My cigarette had gone out by itself, so I lit it again, took a puff as I turned around, dreading the walk back. What I did do was exhaled in relief, just knowing that this person on hold could potentially help me.

"Mam, are you still there?"

I had visualized the operator growing up in some spectacular household with the perfect siblings, mother, father, siblings, and pets. He spoke politely and showed genuine concern about helping me.

"Yes Sir, I'm still here. I'm walking down to the bus station so I can find out the zip code."

"Mam, let's just start with that location, where was that bus station? Do you happen to know the street?"

"Yes, actually. I walked up 7th St. and turned right on Alameda. Now I'm going back down Alameda St., back towards 7th St."

"Okay. Great. Now it looks like we're going somewhere. I know exactly what vicinity you are in. Let's get you started. You need shelter, right? So, I'm going to give you a handful of numbers to jot down, okay? Do you have a pen?"

I wasn't prepared for any of this, which made this moment so fascinating. Not knowing where I would be in the next hour or so was quite suspenseful, but I knew deep down in my spirit I wouldn't be sleeping on the street. I was fearless. In time I reached back to the bus station, dragging my luggage and backing my old, worn out backpack that I apparently stole from my cousin back at Berkeley High without knowing.

There sat a man outside on the steel seating area. He looked like he was waiting on a ride. He didn't look too busy, just sat there looking around while drinking his Pepsi. I figured he had a pen, so I placed my luggage against the bus station's concrete rough white wall, then relieved myself from my backpack. I placed it on an empty seat, flicked my smoke on the ground and proceeded to walk towards this Pepsi guy.

"Excuse me Mr."

He was eyeing the streets and I assumed he didn't hear me.

"Excuse me Mr.! Do you happen to have a pen I could possibly use by any chance? I'll give it right back to you, I promise."

The Pepsi man turned his head right and then looked me up and down.

"Damn baby, yeah, for you. I only got a pen for you sweetheart."

He reached inside of his bag and handed me the pen.

"I got more than that too baby girl, what else you need? Where you comin' from?"

I just didn't have the time to chatterbox because my mind was set on my next step.

"Thanks so much, but I really need to finish this call and write some information down... Bay Area."

I walked away back towards my luggage, grabbed my backpack, and set it beside my leg after I sat down.

"Hello, Sir? I'm sorry about that, I had to get a pen. I'm ready to take the numbers."

"Okay Mam, I have the Mission, Good Shepherd For Women, the Union Rescue Mission...."

He proceeded to give me more numbers. I was so grateful now that I had leads.

"And Mam, the Mission gives out food daily. I would suggest too that you go to the Union Rescue Mission, I hear that they give you up to two weeks or something around that time frame. Also, there is a county building in that area of the Union Rescue Mission. There are a lot of resources in that area. Good luck to you."

"Awesome, thanks so much for helping, take care."

"You do the same, bye bye now."

My adventure began after ending the conversation with the 211 operator. It was time to put those numbers to good use. The first place I called was the Union Rescue Mission. I spoke with a man who told me that I needed to be there by 1:30pm in order to receive a bed ticket. Something unexplainable had to be on my side that day. A bed! I could have a place to sleep tonight, and after my first night, I could stay there for up to fifteen days. Wow! Now we are talking business! Stephan was a volunteer at the Union Rescue Mission who I had spoken with on the phone and whom I met there when I arrived.

The directions beforehand were quite simple; walk up 7th Street, turn right on San Pedro and the Union Rescue Mission would be on my left across the street. All of what I saw was so foreign to me. I had never in my entire life seen this before. The streets were filled with trash. I mean any piece of trash you could think of was there. There was used toilet paper, scraps of old food, beer cans, shopping carts, used condoms, bloody tampons and I even stepped over a needle! Okay, is this like the twilight zone? I really did wonder if I had just walked through some vortex or another planet. Still so unfamiliar, but my curiosity was at its highest point. In addition, I had been completely oblivious to what this really was.

Eventually, I made it inside to the first quaint office area. The person occupying that office directed me down the wide hallway towards the women's section. They had two huge rooms separating the men and the women. I looked around in this recreational area and there were ladies watching T.V and charging up their cell phones. After probing the recreational area, I walked outside and became face to face with Stephen at another quaint office. Stephan was a pretty cool guy. He had long locks and looked nothing like I had imagined over the phone when I spoke with him.

After thirty minutes, my intake process was over and I was given a fifteen-day bed ticket with a bed number. I was so thankful now that I could settle in, take my heavy backpack off, and rest with the women in the recreational area. Dinner was at 5:45pm and you had to show your bed ticket in order to eat. I actually enjoyed the food, but a lot of people complained about it. I didn't understand how someone could complain when it's free food. I just kept my mouth shut and went with the flow because I could tell that some of the women would have no problem with starting some shit. I'm not a fighter, plus I'm skinny and I know I wouldn't have stood a chance.

The cafeteria reminded me of my middle school's cafeteria. It had the same smell. Here I am in Downtown LA, dressed like an updated hippie with my tight patched up skinny jeans, and my hoodie pulled over my head. They even had security patrolling in the cafeteria. One security guard had to constantly tell me to take my hood off, which I thought was a ridiculous idea. I was so used to wearing my hood that it became second nature. By this, the security thought I was being "disobedient". Wow, once again this is so foreign to me. After we ate, the men would have dinner. Typical American culture! I found it ridiculous, but I just went with the flow.

At 7:45pm, we were able to go upstairs to our beds and behold one gigantic room full of bunk beds four feet apart from each other. Holy shit! What the flying fuck! Seventy women plus in one gigantic room! 10:00pm, a residential shelter worker yelled "lights outs." I lied in my number fifty-three bed and listened to conversations from way across the room. There were snores, gas passing, stank from every which way. My nostrils had to bare so much distress. Then again, I just went with the flow and was so thankful that I had a place to lay my head.

Everything was scheduled. In the morning we had to leave at 5:45am. That wasn't an issue; I was an early bird like my mother so I had no confliction. I retrieved some clothes from my luggage, which was kept in storage along with the other women's possessions. After getting dressed, I headed downstairs to charge my phone and come up with a plan for the day. It was too early to go to the county building so I sat in the recreational area and wrote down a handy list of things I needed to do. 7:30am came and I stepped outside into the vortex, walked my little tooshie to the county building, took care of all the paperwork, was on general relief in two weeks, and I received food stamps the next day.

Ten days had gone by and I met a bunch of people in such little time. People would just walk up to me and start conversations. I'm an open person so I engaged in small talk and sometimes I couldn't keep my mouth shut. I befriended a woman named Sophia, she was from Minnesota and had stopped in San Diego for change of life cards, but her plan there didn't work out. Unfortunately, she found herself in Skid Row!

Holy shit, I've heard that before. Wait that's where I am? Told you I had no clue. I cannot believe this shit.

Sophia and I would become somewhat inseparable. We would walk around and try to remember how to get back. I learned my way around quickly. I even took time to read local billboards of job postings, but all I really saw was Skid Row this and Skid Row that. Well, ain't this a bitch, I really am in Skid Row. I had to google it. Terror rushed through my aching bones. In a split second, I was petrified.

I could die here. I could fucking die here. Okay, deep breather, relax it's okay.

Remember when your mother or father said not to walk down those creepy streets when it was too late and to make sure you were with someone at night if possible. Well, imagine that times a trillion. It doesn't need to be night time. The daylight was not an issue for anything to happen. Every ghetto in America could never compare to Skid Row. Please believe that one. I even had to ask someone where I was just to validate my findings.

Once my general relief became available on my EBT (EVEN BETTER THAN) card, I splurged, and by that time I had another friend, Tommy. Tommy and I would walk through the financial district and stop at the liquor store. We'd stack up on as much booze that we needed for the rest of the day. Then we'd ride the Metro drunk without paying, and get stopped by the sheriff and ticketed for not having money on our TAP cards. Tommy was shy, but when he got drunk, he opened up a bit and his face would get real sweaty. It reminded me of play dough. Almost like you could move his cheek up and it could just stay in that position. Our love of alcohol was what brought us together. It bonded us. He was a liar, and I could read through his lies, said he was from Palm Springs when he was from Banning. We still hung anyway.

After my stay at the Union Rescue Mission, I had been referred to a program called Avenues to Work where I had been given a private room with a sink and a mirror at the Russ Hotel on San Julian Street. I would be able to stay there for up to three months. Again something unexplainable had been on my side throughout this journey.

The catch was in order to be a part of the program, you had to partake in twenty-five job searches every week and have completed a list of jobs that were due on every Friday. I had told Sophia about the Avenues to Work program, and she was excited to check it out, but unfortunately she could not get in because the program required a drug screening and she'd had been smoking weed with the goons on San Pedro Street.

For some strange reason, I was nervous to take the drug test. I had been in contact or even high off contact when I went to my cousin's apartment down by Westlake. My cousin's from the Bay Area as well, and he had moved back to LA after a failed attempt that took place years before which I was a part of, but that's a different story. My previous attempt didn't compare to my second. Even knowing that I didn't have anything to worry about, I was still nervous anyhow. I passed with flying colors. Then again, I was lucky they didn't check for alcohol.

There I was, climbing up the status bar in Skid Row, I have my own room, no more crazy conversations to keep me awake. I could chant Nam Myoho Renge Kyo freely. I could light incense when I passed gas. I could go downstairs to the lobby and heat my food in the microwave. I would make rice in a Tupperware bowl, and if I knew I could have made bacon in the microwave then, it would have been bacon. I had no curfew.

From that comfort and the small bits of security, I may have abused my blessing. You weren't supposed to bring alcoholic beverages inside the Russ Hotel if you were in a work program. I did, I did countless times. I drank a lot, in the mornings even before I went on interviews. Something kept saving me time and time again. Thinking back, I could have been in sticky situations. Honestly, I think I had nine lives like a feline. I seriously could have been killed by the Cubans who sold single counterfeit cigarettes imported from Mexico. I tend to talk a whole lot more when intoxicated; maybe I irritated the Cubans with my nonchalant hippie attitude.

My mouth got me in deep shit when I bought a cigarette and decided to hang out in their area where they were making their money. I even sat my ass down in one of their chairs and some guy who was not Cuban told me to leave before it got ugly. I did not listen. Next thing you know, the Cuban man picks up the chair I was sitting in and flicks my skinny ass out of it. I must have become sober that very moment, picked myself up, and stumbled away. While stumbling away, they started speaking in a different language, pointing at me with a look of anger on their faces.

I frequented a bar called the Down and Out, plenty of times. After coming from there pissy drunk, I managed to evade predators. This one night in my room, I was caught by surprise because usually every five minutes I would hear helicopters circling, but something was different, strange. It was quiet. Then all of a sudden I heard a woman scream for help. Then I heard a man telling her to shut up. He was raping her. I couldn't do anything to stop it.

A few people had told me about rapists being almost everywhere in Skid Row, and the police didn't care about some homeless woman getting raped. It was late, I was in shock, and I could not think of what I could possibly do. So I waited until the morning and wondered what happened to that woman who screamed for help, still to this day. Speaking of the police, the LAPD was corrupt and unprofessional. One cop tried his hardest to recruit me sexually. I honestly did not feel protected by law enforcement.

So many times I had made a fool of myself, but managed to work odd jobs. I started working at a homeless shelter while I was still homeless, and at this small time event company. That job got me my apartment at the Alexandria. I quit my job where I was a residential advisor at the shelter. I couldn't take it, and my manager that seemed to be polite became this ghetto ass chick from south central who didn't want to give me my check when I quit. That's when legal aid got involved. Damn right I got my check.

For the most part, I was a functional alcoholic, but my hangovers were like death. Sometimes they lasted for days. Something was seriously wrong, that's when I ended up at Kaiser on Sunset Blvd across from the Scientology church. I could barely walk to the emergency room after leaving the red line metro. I would sober up for a couple of days after recouping, then I would binge and get kicked out for good from my favorite bars with no recollections as to what I did. One of the bouncers at Down and Out told me they had me on video tape doing who knows what, and apparently, the owner didn't want me there. That's what I was told.

A place I performed at called the Last Bookstore had a little trouble with me. One evening, I walked in with a posse of folks drunk, loud, and obnoxious while someone was in the middle of their performance. Then I end up with some woman in the bathroom, smoking cigarettes. Something happened outside the bathroom also, and that was on videotape at the bookstore. Another security guard had told me about that one, some days after the incident.

I swear when I came to my right and sober mind I would try to avoid all people I acted a fool in front of. It was impossible. I lived across the street from the Bookstore and Down and Out was attached to my apartment building. I could literally take my elevator down from the sixth floor to the lobby, turn right and be face to face with the security. Then I would hear, you were so fucked up last night, then I'd just keep walking, feeling embarrassed, I'd run into more people I couldn't remember, they'd stop and talk to me about previous engagements and I'd just look at them in complete bewilderment.

All I wanted was to get to where I was going. My anxiety would creep up, and I'd jot down a corner hoping I wouldn't see any more people, but then I would run into my neighbor Ellis. When I'd run into him , I'd just say fuck it, let's go to Rite Aid. Rite Aid was only a block away from my apartment. Every time I went there I had to have my Merlot just for starters. My cousin that I had spoken of earlier had gotten evicted so we had decided to stay together at the Alexandria. Two fast people living together are like trying to mix oil and water together. It was a very bad combination.

So many people were in and out of this apartment. Our neighbor Ellis stayed on the third floor. That man still is my friend to this day, but he was a wild character. He smoked weed, drank just as much as me if not more. His favorite phrase was "Ohh child"- just imagine a gay man saying it! When we partied together it was an absolute disaster. I could not get away from the madness.

Somehow acquaintances would shimmy their way to my apartment, and my cousin would open the door, keep in mind I was either drunk or hung over. They'd come in with weed, alcohol, molly, coke, you name it. One acquaintance left a suitcase, which I thought was full of clothes, when she took a longer than expected vacation to Las Vegas. I opened the suitcase out of curiosity and found bags of meth, weed, and some other shit. Enough drugs for me to be paranoid forever.

I would think why are we partying on a Monday and I have an interview to go to in the morning. Peer pressure and weakness is a motherfucker. Our window faced Spring Street, and every time the Down and Out bar let out, we hollered at the clubbers in our drunken state, we thought it was hilarious. If someone slept over, it was guaranteed that they would find my empty shot bottles under pillows, side of my bed, behind the T.V, all over the place. Constant company, I was barely alone. Soon as someone left, another one showed up. I had this one neighbor, Mr. Wells; he was an older gentleman who was crazy in his own right. I would go to his apartment one door down and talk with him about all kinds of things. He had relocated some year ago to LA from San Francisco and could relate with me since I was a Bay Area native. Still, I could not escape the alcohol. Everywhere I turned, it was there like an annoying kid! Mr. Wells had some real good wine, I could not help myself. All of our neighbors were a bit odd. Most of them did music, photography, videography, and there were some actors.

Something just had to be happening and where ever it was happening in our apartment building, I was there. I lost plenty of cellphones so many times that I forgot that I needed them. At one point, I had three phones at once, but I only remembered buying one. All three vanished anyway, and I just told people to catch me if you can or email me.

Down our hallway, I had partied with another neighbor, didn't know their name, but there were about fifteen people there drinking and doing drugs. We sat on the floor and talked. People bragged about their up and coming projects blah, blah, blah-the people in LA. Then some folks behind me started sniffing this pink powder shit that had been in pill form until they crushed it. What the hell, my curiosity led me to try it.

After my experiment, I fell sick, went down the hall back to my apartment, bothered my cousin, and went to sleep. The next day I felt horrible, I cried. Whatever that pill was, it made me sick for a whole week. I was drinking Pedialyte, swallowing Benadryls, and nothing was helping. Yes, I went to the emergency, and I think Kaiser got tired of seeing my face. I got tired of seeing my face!

SORRY

Dumb she was
numb she was
stubborn she was
Didn't think about her future or her loved ones
Down her journey she realized she was sorry
Sorry mom, sorry brother, sorry sister
And everyone who found her troublesome
But she made mistakes to learn
Still managed to carry on
Dim room light fixture somewhere placed irregular
Away from the center
Across from that she sat
Alone by herself feeling detached
Not at all home even though that's where she would rest
Countless nights of nightmarish dreams
And that wasn't a place where she wanted to be
The bottles were like medicine curing her but killing her
Managed working in the morning but her day progressed
with shots of guilty coffee

Didn't take it black but brown and she guzzled it down
Hiding behind bathroom doors wrapping up evidence in toilet tissue
Heading back like it wasn't an ongoing issue
Didn't you smell her from afar no one knew
Slick and mischievous
Fifteen minute walk around the block
Heading to the corner store to buy more shots
No care whatsoever
Gulp after gulp
Day is over head home but first must have more
So she could rid the hangover from the morning before
True story
Sorry mom, sorry brother, sorry sister, and everyone who found her troublesome.

GUILT

Aren't you exhausted from waking up with shame and guilt? Maybe you did not wake up. Maybe you never went to sleep. When was the last time you even slept well? Your conscious won't let you have the satisfaction. Your heart is beginning to ache, there is tightness in your throat, you would like to cry, but the tears don't seem to flow. You regret the night before and to make matters worse, you feel like shit and can't figure out what to do with yourself. You have no recollection. Amnesia has dawned on you. You would like to call someone you were with while you were out having a ball, but would you be able to face the demon you let out? You would rather retreat, ignore and pretend like nothing happened.

The irritating buzzing alarm clock hurts your ears and when you reach over to turn it off you knock over your wallet that sat passively on your dusted wooden mini dresser. You silence the alarm, reach for your wallet, open it, and the bills you just retrieved from your account last night are nowhere to be found. In that moment you notice an unbearable pain around your eyebrow. Your trembling fingers detach from your wallet and move towards your brow. There you feel a clump and rugged dried blood. Now you are concerned and can barely swallow your saliva because of dehydration. Racing to your bathroom's mirror would be an arduous task. Remember you couldn't sleep from your inner thoughts creeping in, filling you up like party balloons full of helium with unavoidable shame and guilt. Last night is completely distorted, and you try and pick pieces for this puzzle, but your mind's playing tricks. You can't figure out what's fact and what's fiction.

Maybe I got robbed. Did I lose all my cash? I couldn't have spent my last. Maybe I tripped and fell. I don't remember getting into a fight. Fuck.

Are you ever going to give in and surrender to yourself? You can alleviate unnecessary guilt and shame, stop punishing yourself. You know you have been there before, you know this all too well. You know what it feels like to catch yourself red-handed. You are a fucking burglar, dammit! Stealing days from your life. No pawn shop in the world would want that because it's priceless!

Finally, you use the little energy you have to go to your bathroom, you relieve yourself before looking in the mirror, and your urine is dark and has an unsettling smell. You flush. Now you are facing your mirror and behold! The almighty untouchable addict has been defeated with a TKO from the hands of someone uncharted! How sad. How ridiculous. Now you look even more like a fool. Your thirst subsides after turning on the faucet as you drink the desperately needed H2O. Memories of the life you led before your addiction play over and over again like overplayed songs from the radio.

What happened to me? I used to be happy. I can't even stand up straight. I let my sister down. I loved working out and playing basketball, now I don't even play anymore. I can't stand to see my family when I'm like this. Who are you? What are you doing? I'm losing weight. I look worse than I looked last week. Why are there bags under my eyes? I can't go to my job like this. What will my boss say if I called off? I just called off last week. I have a bottle in my freezer. I forgot about that. No! Don't think about it. I got a good deal on that bottle though. Fuck. How about I call off. Try and sleep. I can't sleep. I can't fall asleep. Who the hell hit me? It's gonna turn black. I'd probably feel better if I drank some of that vodka. No, I won't. Hmm. Maybe I will. No, I won't. Why am I still standing in front of my mirror? Fucking hate my life right now. My head is killing me. Maybe I should shower. I don't have the energy to do that.

After facing yourself in your mirror, your knees collapse, and in seconds you fall to the cold marble bathroom floor. The onset of a breakdown emerges. Inescapable hyperventilation sets in. You are beginning to lose control. Automatically you curl up in fetal position. Sweat trickles down from your scalp, greeting salty teardrops. Temple veins plunge against your flesh. On a scale from one to ten, your head pain would be rated at twenty.

Your cell phone rings and you know who the caller is because of the customized ringtone. Your mother! The thought of her seeing you in such a grave state sends you bawling out enough tears to quench droughts in California during mid summer. The ringing fades as you block out all and everything that's neighboring. There is unquestionably no place to go when you are in the abyss with the exception of moving forward and climbing higher than ever attempted.

Forever changing
None Permanent
Light illuminates the dreary
Glowing radiantly within your euphoric realm

CONSEQUENCE

Consequence: That which follows from any act, cause, principle, or series of actions; an event or effect produced by some preceding act or cause; a result, (Webster's New Twentieth Century Dictionary, Second Edition).

Hello? Did we not think it would come to this? Do not lie, you were not thinking rationally. Your high can only last so long; it's covered your oozing wound like a Band-Aid without any Neosporin. Let's talk accountability and responsibility- wait, oh yes, the inevitable consequences. Quite scary! Are you feeling guilt? Maybe you'd rather pretend you are invisible. You might want to procrastinate before you walk out your front door and notice, dude where's my car? Towed, impounded away with the others. Once a star, well-appreciated employee, but now you are slacking, your performance just isn't up to par. You don't even know what bus to take to work. You can't rent a car. You have a DUI now! Now it's cigarette after cigarette, exhaling all your frustration. Your inner voice is beginning to annoy you. Constant thoughts of

what if I, I should have, what am I going to do, why the hell did I, fuck I'm so stupid, I'm gonna get fired, I'm already short on rent.

    Shut up inner voice! No sympathy here, your job doesn't care, remember you are not that star employee anymore. There are plenty of stars in the sky. You can be replaced next week, how about that? Probably sooner. It's all too familiar, the stress is too much to bare, and you radiate with magnetic energy that connects you with your vice. 360 degrees, the cycle continues. You still haven't learned your lesson. Despite what's at stake, you have managed to spend your last on your so called remedy. Your livelihood could slip away so easily. You would be left behind waiting for the last train to some desolate island in some country you can't even pronounce. Too bad you are an adult and did all this to yourself. Now you are smothered in deep, dark depression. When will you man or woman up, for goodness sake, hold your own and be accountable for your actions? Right now, I'm hoping.

    My irrational thinking led me to say and text the most rude, hateful, judgmental things. It also brought me lonesome, lost relationships, and numerous cigarette packs. My name became synonymous with my "bad habit". Choose your path wisely and with caution. In the "Addiction Would Have You" poem, there is a stanza that talks about being invincible when you are deluded with toxic substances. There have been countless situations where I actually felt like superwoman and couldn't be touched. Boy, was I wrong. Tell me who in their right mind treats the police as if they were a taxi cab?

    Good luck had been on my side in previous successful attempts, but one day that good luck vanished.

Guess where I ended up? That's right I ended up in the Santa Rita Jail for public intoxication. I was stunned. This happened outside of the Wal-Mart parking lot. Moments beforehand, I'd been inside Wal-Mart parading around sneaking sips of my Mickey's 24-ounce beer while helping customers pick out Christmas presents for whomever. My ride that brought to Wal-Mart, disappeared, and I searched frantically to find them, but to my amazement I was stuck.

No money, drunk, I was even lost. I had no clue to where I was. That's when I saw the police slowly driving, and my first thought was that they could take me to my grandmother's house because they took me home in Los Angeles some months before so I figured I'd give it another shot. There I was flagging the Oakland police down for my stranded engagement. They stopped, got out of their vehicle, and told me to sit on the curb. Next thing you know, I'm in handcuffs. Real tight handcuffs that left red marks on my tiny wrists.

They asked the most idiotic questions and I answered sarcastically, *"Of course officer I have been drinking that's why I need you and your partner to take me to my grandmother's house which I believe isn't that far from here."*

Good grief! The backseats of police vehicles are nothing nice. I chatted with the officers the entire drive to Santa Rita. They didn't even read me my Miranda rights, they also didn't breathalyze me. I guess it was that noticeable. Maybe I asked for the joyride to jail. Upon arriving at the Santa Rita jail, the freezing temperature hit my skin like the onset of hypothermia. It was ice cold, uncomfortable, not to mention I was three days into my menstrual. At least I did not starve, but my sandwich was thrown to me like a ball to a dog.

I didn't complain, not even once. I did have conversations with the working officers in the jail, I even recited a poem when they had us "inmates" stand against the white wall while they patted us down. They made me take off my shoes and socks and stand on that disgusting floor barefoot. There was leftover dried blood on the wall where I had to place my hands while I "spread them". 2 Pac's "How Do You Want It?" played at a suitable tone lingering from one of the officer's office. I'm being punished with the raps of 2Pac!

In my drunken state, I had found my situation to be ridiculously insanely hysterical. However, when I came down and the disturbing hangover set in, sheer panic pumped through my veins. Disbelief multiplied by a hundred. How am I going to fix this one? I have a clean, crisp background. I had never been to jail before! I tried my hardest to sleep my panic away, but there were several women in one tiny cell. For the most part, they talked about nonsense. One woman came in some time after my arrival. She was high and we became cell friends showing off our raunchy tattoos to one another.

Suddenly, my last name was called and I was being discharged at 4:30 in the morning. A few floors down, I was greeted by a clerk who gave me back my prized possessions, along with a sheet of paper that had my charge and court date. Unbelievable, I thought, but I'm an adult and I have to take care of my business even when it's inconvenient. Our complex system once again, there is no output without an input.

Circumstances like these can add fuel to a burning flame. Self-pity does not get you far. Why spend time looking at the ground when the whole wide beautiful world could be in clear view? It's easy on the eyes. We must begin to understand and learn from our actions. Make adjustments when it's absolutely necessary. Did we not learn about this in our adolescence? Maybe, maybe not. Wrong from right was instilled in my subconscious, but somehow I chose not to abide, and by not abiding I fell victim to massive destructive behavior. I could blame my mother for her mental and emotional abuse she inflicted upon to me, but that would not help much; believe me I have tried and failed horribly doing so.

You cannot get through a locked door if no one's home. You can knock all you want, but it's guaranteed that nobody will answer. What I am saying correlates with the outside sources that we attempt to fix, when the inside needs to be healed and remedied. Let's solve the problem before it starts. And... How do we do that? We open our brains, and come to a realization that what we are doing and have been doing is not working! Grow up! Begin to love yourself wholeheartedly. You are special! Every day you have so many options to choose from. It is a matter of choosing the correct one. Everything will start to flow smoothly. Haven't you had enough of those raging white waters? Don't you want a smooth sailing ship so you can continue to be the captain that you are in your life right now?

I know I am capable.

I see and feel my inner strength.

There is nothing I cannot do.

Every new day is different than the last.

I create new possibilities as I go.

STRENGTH

Strength: The state or quality of being strong; force; power, vigor, the power to resist strain, stress, etc. Toughness, durability, (Webster's New Twentieth Century Dictionary, Second Edition).

    Let's delve deeper and develop our hibernating strength. You would be surprised at your fight or flight responses if you were in a situation where you had to decide whether to live or die. If you become complacent and fill your brain with depleting, negative thoughts then you are preparing yourself for doomsday. Strength, I am not referring to a blow or a punch to a rib. Anybody could do that, that's easy! If you have immense muscle mass, then of course, no problem you can take down your squirming opponent. However, the strength I am indicating is inner strength, mental capability.

    It is mind over matter. Point blank. Period. Use your brain pinky! They lied to you and you believed every single untruthful statement they boldly uttered. Statements like *you could never do that, you're not that smart, you'll never have as much money as me*. They shot you down when they could not see the unseen. Your hidden quality lies on the opposite side of weakness. It is time to peel off dysfunctional lies and face the truth of who you really are. Let's begin to function at our strongest mental level. You will heal, just as your skin grows back after a scrape against a concrete surface.

Your life is magical. Think of all your hardships you have already conquered. Your strength does lie in your previous experiences. The saying is what doesn't kill you only makes you stronger. I believe that to be true. While in the midst of the struggle, hold tight onto your faith, have faith in yourself. Do not think, you must certainly know that you are limitlessly great, stronger than any muscle in the human anatomy. Become self-sufficient while learning how to maintain your patience and focus. If you changed overnight, that would be a miracle! However, most of us must do the strenuous work to aid in our well-being. Time does not wait for anyone! You are capable right this minute! Do not wait while your life clock continues to pass twelve. We can dream and fantasize about how good our future could be, but that dream will not be actualized without the necessary steps and actions.

Let's appreciate ourselves! Acknowledge every positive trait that you possess, for doing this could propel you steps forward and create a day full of joy. Each day, love yourself a little more. Be thankful that you have your eyesight, your legs are still working, and you can still get around and enjoy other's company. If you can't see then be thankful for your guide dog and guiding stick. If you can't walk be thankful for your wheelchair even though one wheel may be a little bit rusty. Stop complaining and bring forth self-love and appreciation! You are becoming a witness to your inevitable growth and reemerging strength. Embrace your liberation immediately! Provide a clear concrete guide with practical individualized goal setting to help you become organized. Remember you are strong. With each day your strength increases drastically!

BREAKING THE CYCLE

When I was fourteen years old, I found three crack rocks on my grandmother's bathroom sink. My hand hovered over the toilet as I attempted to discard them by flushing them. Before I could follow through, my father started banging on the locked door, furious as to what I might do with his crack rocks. He kept banging rapidly in his manic episode. I stood there weeping, tears slid down my mountain checks like the Augrabies Falls in South Africa.

Eventually, I opened the door, and he rushed in, grabbing his crack from my hand. I knew he was on drugs, but I had never seen that side of him before. I was used to him being drunk, that was the norm. Every time I saw my father he had a beer, his newspaper and the T.V turned on and tuned into ESPN. JB Brown, he didn't have a middle name, but he was influenced by some news anchor by the name Emerald, which he named me after as my middle name, but spelled it with an I, and not an E. My father had been known by many from Compton, California to the Bay Area. I remember walking down streets in Berkeley and being stopped at random, "Are you J.B's daughter, you look just like him?"

Even youngsters would know my dad and would call me little J.B. Drugs and alcohol turned him into a monstrous being. I had heard stories about him beating my mother. I never saw that take place. Maybe I did, but I was too young to remember, or I just blocked it out from my memory. What I do recall is him bashing his at the time girlfriend in her face. I was twelve when that happened in my grandmother's two-bedroom apartment in Berkeley on Channing Way. I had been sleeping on the beige love seat couch when I woke up to Irene Lu screaming. My dad was on top of her, plunging his fist into her frightened face. Helplessness soaked the living room until I yelled out "Daddy, stop!" He then looked at me and calmly stopped attacking. My grandmother had been asleep in her bedroom and did not know what had happened. I was in shock and could not understand fully what I just witnessed.

For the most part, I looked up to my father despite all the negative that surrounded his aura. Some days were good, some days were ugly. I never lived with him, but he came around sometimes and called when he was in jail. I was fine with that. He'd call me on the fifth of September, and wish me happy birthday, and I'd tell him -*I was born on the sixth, but I'll take what I can get from you, Daddy.*

He was proud of me and had my first album cover glued to his wall in his apartment. I'd visit him and his crack head friends would answer his door while he was upstairs. His ashtray reeked and was always full of butted cigarettes, half-smoked joints and whatnot. He'd always say the craziest things. One birthday he let me throw a party. I had turned fifteen. All of my friends from Berkeley High came. My father had been with a new woman and they both partied with us young folks while they were loaded off some shit. His apartment was packed inside, oh and yes let's not forget to mention the party goers outside in the front yard. The music was blasting and out of nowhere my father presses pause on the stereo. Everyone stops dancing and all you can hear is chatter amongst my friends.

Then my Dad starts talking, slurring his words and says "I like pussy so much, my daughter came out liking pussy! HA CHA CHA! Powered on out to the max! Kool-Aid ass muthafuckas!" My friends all laughed, and afterward most came up to me saying that my dad was a cool dude. I was tipsy myself, so I didn't care about what my father just said, it was true anyway. I just laughed at the situation and kept dancing when he turned the music back on. I was accustomed to his sporadic behavior.

When I'd run into him on the streets while I was with friends, he'd grab his balls, shake them, and say, "you know where you came from? You came from my balls, my balls!" I'd just calmly reply with *"I know Daddy, I know."* Then he would give me five dollars and walk away while telling me to tell my mother he said hi. What a character!

He was tall and slender, green-eyed and high yellow. There is a picture I have of him when he was a kid. At times I'd look at it and wonder what the hell happened to his innocence. I inherited most of his traits. Alcoholism runs through my veins. It's still amazing that I turned out not as bad as him. Considering he did crack before I was born, and probably was high off crack during my mother's conception. I have managed to defy all odds; my Father was an example for me to turn my life around.

That turning point took years, crashed cars, shattered home windows, slit wrists, and numerous pills swallowed. While in the midst of it all, it's unnoticeable that you are reenacting what you subconsciously learned in your adolescence. At first you are curious, and then you are influenced not only by your peers, but television shows, music, popular culture, and the entire media as a whole. Constantly reminded with advertisements of the latest new improved formulated alcoholic beverage.

It starts off slow and it's a shit load of fun! It's new! You like how you feel because it's different. It brings suspense and it's daring. Excitement flairs up and you begin to feel like you are the coolest person on the planet. After time passes, you become use to it, and it's nothing like how it used to be, but you still do it because you made it a "habit" a... "bad habit" at that.

There is still love left. At the end of the day when you are fed up, lost, and terrified. The solution is there, you just have to wipe those nasty boogers from your eyes and look just a little closer. Look under the surface. This vice is not your identity. Understand that the cycle must and will be broken. I went a whole year without calling the coroner's office when my father passed away. Simply because I was so afraid that they would tell me that he had overdosed. When I did come to a conclusion that I was ready, I was told he had had a heart attack.

He was young, but his lifestyle contributed to his demise. My mother passed two years later. Again, her lifestyle triggered her heart attack as well. She didn't do drugs, but her drinking became out of control which led to our dysfunction as mother and daughter. My problem grew bigger when she'd leave jugs of wine in the refrigerator. Days she would send me to the liquor store to get her drink and my drink, I enabled her, she enabled me. That's why it's extremely vital to not put yourself in hazardous predicaments that will send you back to Level 1, drowning. It's hard to stay afloat, but it is not impossible. Break from this cycle, and continue in a straight or curved line to genuine freedom. There will be struggles but you're equipped to fight and win this battle.

REHAB, "THE HAB"

I had learned grounding exercises in rehab and from time to time I now find myself paying close attention to where my feet are planted. Interestingly enough I lived with 15 women from different backgrounds and the house ran smoothly as peanut butter on enriched bread. That was a joke. Problems ranged from alcoholism to coke and crack.

I saw women come and leave. I became really good friends with someone who had just gone through hell as she ended up in jail from her substance abuse induced psychosis. She had set fire to a vending machine after trying to communicate with it telepathically. No answer so a fire spread, but was put out soon after. She was taken to jail and released on her own recognizance and later transferred to our rehabilitation program. There was me, the quiet listener withholding precious input. I was surely uncomfortable as I thought that everyone was overly emotional. Yet, I found out that I was a bundle of emotional tornadoes. I learned that the way I was brought up was unhealthy for my emotional well-being and by talking with an onsite therapist would be beneficial to the realization of how my childhood affected me as an adult.

  We had to be awake before 7 am, and a worker woke everyone up sometimes at 6am, other times 6:20 am, or whenever she felt best. I thought it was bizarre to wake us up, since we were there to learn skills and be independent and that did the opposite. At 7am, we had silent breakfast and a lot of clients considered the silent breakfast as punishment. Which some staff there made it seem that way as they would stand up with their arms crossed, waiting to see if someone would break the rule of silence. That made me uncomfortable, but I was focused on what I showed up there for.

  The drama was never ending, I couldn't understand why some people were so eager to talk about someone so badly when they couldn't see themselves for what they were, which was an addict just like the other person they talked about. My tolerance stretched and I developed more perspective of others' situations.

  We had three groups in a day regularly and one AA and NA meeting throughout the week. I began to hate the serenity prayer as it was said in unison, but I respected the way of the program. Groups covered co-occurring disorders, self-esteem issues, healthy relationships, living skills, processing of grief, seeking safety, which is a counseling model that focuses on helping people attain safety from trauma or substance abuse, sometimes both. To conclude my list, relapse prevention was where we came up with a plan to combat our addictions, and then there was the feelings group. I opened my shell and I spoke up in a room of 15 other women. I became vulnerable, expressed myself, and feedback was offered to me by the women. Conflict management was seldom an interest for me, but the information was really helpful.

  What I highly recommend is ongoing therapy. I had never had therapy for reasons speculated to me because of my upbringing and my culture pretty much had a stigma attached to therapy. I found it to be very helpful and I had realized how much my childhood had affected me to my core. I deeply believe that it is so much better to let things out that are bothering you then letting it build up because the built up tension can cause dis-ease. I don't regret checking myself in. There is no shame attached to it. I did what I thought was best for me. It was a great learning experience and refreshing of values that I had either forgot about or chose not to bring to the light out of my bullheadedness.

Also, it wasn't just rehab that changed me completely. It's taken thousands of miles to get to this place where I am. My journey wouldn't have been possible without me being curious. I realized that my creative brain could not just be limited, so I wandered into how perception, image, and pre-judgements of someone can automatically have them put into rigidly inflexible titled categories. Some of which can be degrading, offensive, and some may not have any emotional effect simply because we have not challenged that titled category to be anything but what it already is.

We haven't stepped outside the box of identification, identification with the half truth. Yes, I may be an alcoholic, but I'm many other things, but ultimately one thing in particular that can't be fully grasped. Outrageously amazing, I think to be so proud of your occupation's title that you completely forget if YOU ever were proud to be YOU, to begin with. Doctor, pedestrian, soldier, student, inmate, underprivileged, veteran, father, mother, sister, aunt, homeless, pretty girl, rich boy, employee, alcoholic, meth head, coke head, crack head, preacher, officer, teacher, and so forth. It is the surface level of what could be truth, semi-truth, or false made up bullshit. This labeling is always true to someone who actually believes it.

The question- "who are you?" is frightening when you really ponder upon it, especially if you've been told you're worthless or you're nothing but an alcoholic that won't amount to anything special. We tend to think that our parents made us who we are, which is semi-truth. Genetically, yes, they really did, but our environment has played an enormous role. *So does my parents' background make me who I am? Would I be more satisfied with life if I knew my complete family tree so I have a feeling of connectedness? Am I my largest organ, why am I categorized by my skin which isn't the color black, but a caramel brown?* Brown or black doesn't define who I am.

I could list countless adjectives or even hand write them, but that would be just a waste of ink and paper. However, if I were to do that, then from that piece of paper what makes those adjectives meaningful and useful? What gives them life? Does this flesh, breaths, and rhythmic heartbeat along with the descriptive word list make me who I am? Bewilderment rearranges my facial features as I sink into the abyss in thought. Once again who am I and who are you? What do you identify with? The deeper you dig beyond the flesh the closer you are to finding who you really are.

What I am not is that hopeless alcoholic, my sexual organs, my breast, the blondish tiny baby hairs lining the rim of my scalp, the big hairy irregularly round mole inches above my stretched marked buttocks, or the childhood scars that may or may not be a figment of my imagination. However, they are still stamped on my skin like a received unopened postal envelope, which still doesn't say a lot about who I am. Our shells conceal something so vast, something that I believe is so brilliantly outstanding. Our shells are "storytellers" validating typical stereotypes by the staring eye. It isn't their fault for their mental predisposition. Their nurture defined you. Their belief, their knowing, but what is the difference between believing and knowing?

So, should I be upset with the lies that my shell tells? Let me expand on "shell". It's too simplistic at this very moment. The broader view of our shell being our skin, brain, pretty nails, piercing eyes, any part of you that's not connected. Connected to what? When you let go of the physical, when you stop being so concerned about the outer image you begin to uncover who you are. You can not judge my spirit, which is ever pure. Imagine soul to soul insults, what would be insulted? What would be looked down upon? At a higher level, we can start to look at one another and spiritually feel that familiar connection that we once lost due to societal upbringing. Societal upbringing has brought us far and beyond who we really are. Human beings. Yes, half truth. Storytelling.

After the cellular level lies the soulular level. You are a soul. A reflection of the vast universe that is capable of the unknown. Your shell is the container, the protector if you will. However, the power of your spirit or your soul is so strong that it bulges out reaching places far and wide. The containment is not enough, nowhere near as powerful as your boundless real self. Understanding this is difficult simply because we learned differently through nurture, and didn't pay close attention to nature and how it plays a part in our function and the universe.

We are the beings of soulular level oneness through connection. It's really a fantastic realization, just as you realize you have a problem with a toxic substance, the realization and awareness set you free. If nothing else, it's magical, Let this be the magical life altering moment. Now it's a matter of belief or knowing. How do you believe or how do you know? That's really the easy part. You don't have to try, just feel, it's instinctual.

"Either write something worth reading or do something worth writing"

-Benjamin Franklin

ENVIRONMENT

Some may say the people you associate with depict your nature. I would not agree simply because we are individuals with our unique personalities. However, we can be influenced or swayed in both negative and positive fashions. After you have conditioned yourself, you would be ready to protect yourself in potentially dangerous circumstances. As long as you have a sense of solid self, then the environment you are in does not matter, right? That picture could be underdeveloped.

If your environment is unhealthy that would have an affect on you especially if you are recovering and still fighting for more change in your life. Living in a fixed environment could be difficult. Instead of hanging out at your usual places, try finding a new hobby. Something that is productive and engaging. Stress can trigger impulses, if things are too much to bear, then walk away. Take a breathing break if you can. Visit unseen areas in your neighborhood, window shop, or meet new people in a community marketplace. It is time to create a new environment adjusted on your behalf, and away from the detrimental environment at home. The world has so much to offer, and if you are inquisitive you should already be enthusiastic about what's out there that you have not seen or touched yet.

Do not limit yourself. Stay focused on your objective and well-being. You are moving swiftly ahead, others are at a standstill. Through your recovery, you would be able to do things you never thought were possible. All the layers you have shed will renew and replenish you. All the heavy baggage has been reduced to a minimum.

As soon as we walk out into our community, all eyes are on us. However, you are able to walk down streets confidently and proudly because of all the hurdles and obstacles you have managed to conquer. Throughout your day, you have impacted lives silently without even noticing. Your presence could shine through a room. Instead of talking about how you could or would get better, the results are in and you have proof. Stagnant acquaintances may take heed and become curious about what you are doing. You can create a domino effect! How wonderful would that be?

AMAZING LIFE

Either visualize or have faith

Either propel or brake

But if you do fall

Muster up the courage to keep moving forward

Ahead is beautiful, did they not tell you?

You are great!

When you think of your passion, you turn hot red and you shake

Some can see, some are blind, some are ignorant, you are hard to define

Rewire your fate in each minute in time

Somewhere in-between your chest cavity

Listen to your life force

What drives you? Written articles, sheet music, poems and tunes

Risk everything and know that this flower will eventually bloom

Forget everything irrelevant that they ever mentioned to you

Honestly, they just want to be you

Possess the essence and substance that you carry

But that is your gift

Nurture and protect it, shield it from enemies and everything alike

You are amazing, you have an amazing light

You are amazing, you have an amazing life

BRIGHTER DAYS

There are beautiful days and soundless sleeping nights awaiting you. All of which you have struggled time and time again will mold you. Your story could save a life. The darkness fades with light that you shed amongst it. Your distorted truth begins to unravel into a whole truth. It becomes clearer. Throughout years, you have created a fictional character. Someone far removed from your true self. It may be difficult putting lost puzzle pieces back into the unfinished puzzle, but you know that you are more than capable.

How great would it be to be functional? How awesome it would be to enjoy life and experience the simple things without being deluded. Through sobriety comes a clear day. I remember the mist and the heavy fog that barricaded me in my unwavering sickness. Finally, I can hold on to a check! There were plenty of checks that went through the roof. They disappeared! I had nothing to show for it, except for dreaded hangovers and empty bottles. I had to be in that place of burning hell in order to be in a much better place. I had to find myself without the help of a high-tech tracking device. So many setbacks, mistakes and missed opportunities. I was a complete fool!

At times I was aware of my foolishness, but could not control my ugly behavior. I wanted to run away from every single problem I had created. While running, the liquid ran from the bottles. This created even more problems in my life. It is such a dark place being held captive by yourself. Although my thoughts slip into past failures and I drift off thinking if I only didn't do what I did I would have this and I would have that, that way of thinking can lead to unwanted disappointment and depression. The past came and went. No one can change what used to exist. There is no need to dwell on past circumstances.

Be thankful that you made it as far as you are. I have noticed that friends fall off the edge of the Earth. Some people are so stuck in their ways and the only way to accept someone's change is to stay away and keep doing what they are used to doing. As long as you are happier and healthier in your life, that should only matter. Remember you are doing yourself great good.

Validation from outside sources is not the prize. You validate for yourself. The new you will surprise a ton of people. Some will genuinely be ecstatic for you. Some will secretly wish you were at the rock bottom. They will even continue to talk dirt on your beautiful name, making your seemingly problem their own because they have nothing better to do with their miserable lives. Forget them, but wish them happy days and longevity. You have all you need right now. You can change your perception about your life right now. You already have imagined a better life. You must take steps to manifest what you have imagined.

Every waking morning gives rise to a new opportunity. You have to respond quickly and steer the ship back towards shore. People will unquestionably doubt you. Let their disbelief fuel your ambitious gas tank. Even the unthinkable can become the doable and possible. Only you can feel that knocking urge of will simmering. Think positively, reassuring that you are more than capable. There is no success or failure without trying. Also, you will never know what is on the opposite side if you never attempt. How displeasing it would feel to lie in your deathbed wondering about the unseen and untouched? I've been told numerous times that I could not do something by strangers and even people who were dearly close to me.

I was hurt and disappointed for sharing my goals and plans for the future. I received negative feedback. However, that did not stop me in my tracks. Others may have set limits and are confined in their restricted limited thinking. They tend to think more of the usual versus the unusual. The eccentric or off the map way of living is rejected or taboo. It could be because of the unknown elements.

Most of us are afraid to even tamper with it simply because of how we are raised or what we have become so accustomed to seeing every day. Think, dream, act outside the "usual box"! Some things can never be done without being judged, or negatively reviewed. Some people are astonishingly quick on the judgment of elemental flaws, almost like a game of who can point out the most flaws wins the Grand Critic's Flaw award. Negativity seems to attract more attention than positivity. As long as you are seeing the whole picture and believing in yourself, you are on the right track. Open yourself up to being magnificent! You critique your actions and outcomes. Find out what you can change and adjust to flow better.

Be accepting to yourself and let go ego. Truthfully, examine your patterns that may lead you to places where growth is arduous to come by. Begin to understand the pathological role that has impacted your life, showing up through addictive behaviors. This means working a whole lot harder. You absolutely have to rearrange and throw out all the unwanted hoarded items in your life's closets. The baggage is too much to bear! I believe you move a lot swifter with less. Freedom is calling for you! Do you hear freedom's sweet voice? Aren't you curious about what it's like to be free, to have control, and be in awesome great health? This is a work in progress!

I am still fighting to get up and eat a full healthy breakfast. I still want to go out, run, and work on my love handles! One thing is certain, I do not miss being hung over. My whole day would be lousy! All the energy I had only took me to the refrigerator to grab something to eat. The food would come right up some time later. I don't miss the hot and cold spells, or the rapid heartbeat that had me thinking I was going into cardiac arrest! I hated the shaking that I could not control. The clouded slow thinking had me avoiding conversations and people period.

So many days held under in darkness, I missed the simple things like saying hello to wonderful people. My attitude was unacceptable. I would be extremely irritable, building up tension in my body. I was creating another hell within hell itself. Sleeping next to large jugs of water, a take-out container of food from the previous night with annoying house flies hovering over and eventually landing on the last pieces of my T-bone steak from Denny's. Who was that person? I don't think I will ever really know who that person was. That person was completely complicated, making life so difficult. If I ever saw that person again, I'd probably slap the dumb off of their face! How awful that person treated their body. How disrespectful that person was to others. Most of all how disrespectful to the person that reflected in the mirror. It is mind blowing that people actually put up with the madness. Eventually, they did become fed up and never wanted anything to do with that madness.

There were scars and bruises, the blackouts and embarrassments, the want to become invisible, and the anger that poured when you came to terms that you were in fact not invincible. Walking down streets, carrying heavy bags of shame, disbelief, guilt, and feelings of being alone while going through what you are going through alone, floods pavements. You look up and see people enjoying life, doing what you would like to be doing, and the pain begins to become overwhelming. Throughout the crowd, someone was out there feeling your pain. They were trying to focus on their day, but their heavy bags weighed in on them too. Public places made you feel less than because everybody seemed to be doing better than you.

There goes the Whole Foods buying mom and eating only organic veggies, and fruit. There goes the college graduate, the 24 Hour Fitness Zumba teacher, the eccentric Yogi that eats carrots and celery for lunch!

There you are with all that baggage. Who knows, the Whole Foods mom could have a bunch of crack cocaine in her purse next to her daughter's baby wipes! At least you even thought about changing despite the failed actions to do so before. Nothing ever happens without an idea. I feel disgusting thinking back about how I'd show up for business but had play on my brain already. Taste buds full of 40% alcohol, and how no one could notice, amazes me in the worst way. My outer appearance saved me. Inside, I was crumbling like broken cookies in plastic wrapping.

These scars will stay forever, but the room to heal on the inside is still available. Once checked in, you might want to extend your stay. Growth is necessary. Please continue on your path to your happiness. The journey awaits you! I'm wishing you tremendous accomplishments, excellent health, and purity. **Good luck.**

ABOUT THE AUTHORS

J.I. Brown is a native of Berkeley and Oakland, California. J.I. Brown grew up writing poetry, which led to songwriting and storytelling. Over the years, J.I. Brown has produced a variety of songs, released albums, and is now breaking into the literary world with this debut adroit, yet compellingly, fresh, hard-hitting book about personal struggles, alcoholism, drug abuse and the impact it has made. J.I. Brown is currently entwined in multiple endeavors, artistically and professionally.

R.K. Chohan grew up in Livingston, California and attended University of California, Berkeley receiving a BA in Molecular Cell Biology. R.K Chohan later received her Master of Social Work at California State University, Stanislaus. R.K. Chohan's passions include the arts, education, research, and healing through compassion and creativity.

www.ingramcontent.com/pod-product-compliance
Lightning Source LLC
Chambersburg PA
CBHW030222170426
43194CB00007BA/829